# Teacher's Guide

## For Teaching English as a Second Language

### by Gudrun Freese

Consultant and originator of Letterland: Lyn Wendon

# Contents

# Chapter 3: Lesson Plans 33

# Beyond a-z... 74

# Chapter 4: Appendices 81

# Glossary 112

# Index 113

# Foreword

The idea of producing a special version of my Letterland system, tailor-made for teachers of English as a Second Language (ESL) has been close to my heart for some time.

Many ESL teachers have used existing Letterland materials with great success, making their own vocabulary adjustments to suit the needs of their students. But I wanted to give them more support and make them more successful more quickly. The materials that have resulted retain the most successful aspects of the original Letterland phonics programme, but this teaching is combined with basic English Language Teaching (ELT).

Remaining at the heart of Letterland ELT are the powerful pictogram characters, blending abstract letters with people, animals and objects. These Letterlanders allow the shapes and sounds of the English alphabet to be safely introduced to even very young ESL children. At the same time, they also act as focal points for a natural beginner's vocabulary.

We trust that with these special new ELT materials, your students will go from strength to strength because they are learning twin skills: how to crack the code of written English, even as they learn spoken English.

Do write to me at **info@letterland.com**
and let me know how you get on!

*Lyn*

Lyn Wendon
Originator of Letterland

# ★★★ Chapter 1 ★★★

# Introduction

For young learners!

## What is Letterland ELT?

**Letterland ELT** is a starter level course that introduces beginners to:

★ A basic English vocabulary of common words and structures

★ The shapes and sounds of **Aa - Zz**, short and long vowels, **sh** and **ch**

★ Early word-building

★ Listening and speaking skills

## Is Letterland ELT for you?

Our years of correspondence with Letterland teachers in ELT situations have helped us to arrive at the conclusion that...you're all different! Some of you:

★ see your students every day

★ see your students once a week

★ follow a purely activity-based approach

★ use books and CD's

★ speak English as a first language

★ speak English as a second language

★ speak the home language of your students

**Letterland ELT** is flexible, so you can make the decisions on which products you use for your specific circumstance. The full Letterland ELT range is designed to be best suited to teaching phonics and literacy skills in ESL environments.

## Structure of this Teacher's Guide

This Teacher's Guide has four chapters:

1. Introduction          2. Training          3. Lesson Plans          4. Appendices

★ The Training chapter explains in detail how to teach each Section in the Lesson Plans. It will help you to get the best results from your Letterland teaching. Use it to train yourself and other teachers.

★ The Lesson Plans contain seven Sections (See pages 6 and 7)

★ The Appendices contain an Activity Bank and photocopiables, including *Student Cards*, assessment *Activity Sheets*, and *Pupil Record Sheets*.

## Structure of the Lesson Plans

### (1) Present the keyword

Present a simple word that starts with the target sound.

### (2) Letter sound

Introduce the character and 'discover' their letter sound. Teach their action and sing the ELT *Alphabet Song*. Picture-code the plain letter.

### (3) Character words

Learn three words that start with the target sound. Use them in games and simple sentences.

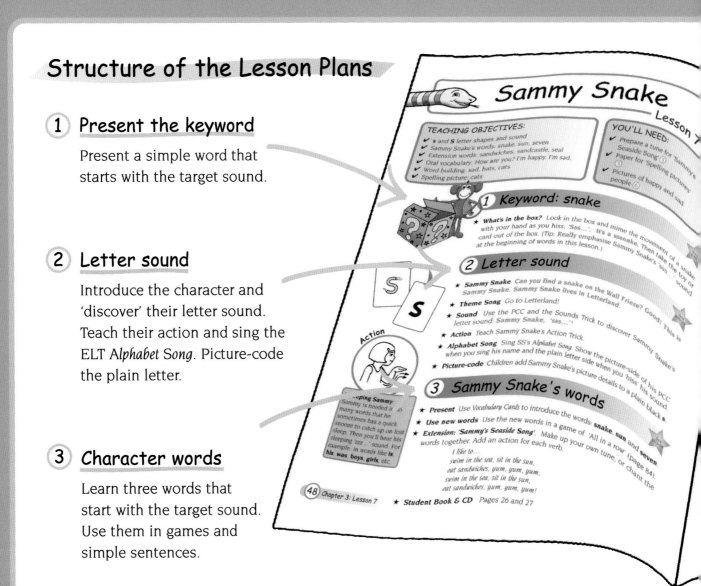

The page numbers in the star next to each Section heading refer you to the relevant pages in the Training chapter. Refer to these pages whenever you need a reminder of how to teach that Section.

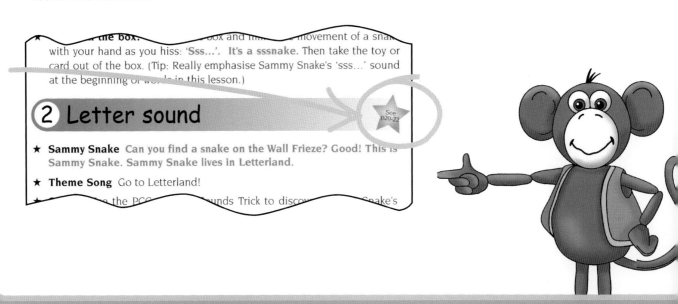

★ ...the box: ...box and ...movement of a snake with your hand as you hiss: 'Sss...'. It's a sssnake. Then take the toy or card out of the box. (Tip: Really emphasise Sammy Snake's 'sss...' sound at the beginning of words in this lesson.)

### (2) Letter sound

See p.20-22

★ **Sammy Snake** Can you find a snake on the Wall Frieze? Good! This is Sammy Snake. Sammy Snake lives in Letterland.

★ **Theme Song** Go to Letterland!

★ ...the PCC ...unds Trick to disco... ...nake's

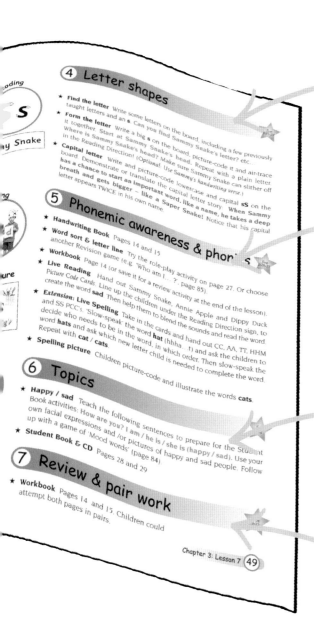

## 4 Letter shapes

Activities for encouraging visual discrimination and letter formation skills. Introduce lower case and capital letter shapes.

## 5 Phonemic awareness & phonics

Activities for developing phonemic awareness and speaking skills. Review previously learnt words and letter sounds. (Some lessons include a phonics / word-building activity.)

## 6 Topics

Activities to help children learn, use and remember common words and structures (grouped in topics).

## 7 Review & pair work

Children complete the review and speaking activities in the *Workbook*, either in pairs or individually.

Each Lesson Plan contains at least 90 minutes of material. It is designed to be flexible so you can chose the activities that suit your needs best. (See page 33)

## Scripted text

Throughout this *Teacher's Guide*, the **bold blue** text provides examples of how you might present key grammatical structures consistently in your lessons, so that they become part of the children's listening vocabulary. **Bold grey** text provides information that you may like to translate – but this is optional, additional information.

## Scope & sequence

| Lesson | Letter | Character's words (Keyword in **bold**) | Topics / speaking vocabulary | Word-building (phonics) |
|---|---|---|---|---|
| 1 | c | **cat**, car, cake | one, two, three | |
| 2 | a | **apple**, ant, acrobat | eyes, nose, mouth; red, green, yellow | |
| 3 | d | **duck**, dog, dinosaur | four, five six, seven; (1-7); father, mother, sister, brother | dad |
| 4 | h | **hat**, house, horse | eight, nine; (1-9); This is my… / These are my… | |
| 5 | m | **magnet**, milk, monkey | I'm hungry. Eat. I'm thirsty. Drink; (1-9) | |
| 6 | t | **telephone**, tiger, ten | ten (1-10); How many fingers? | cat, hat, mat |
| 7 | s | **snake**, sun, seven | How are you? I'm happy / sad. | sad, cats, hats |
| 8 | i | **ink**, insect, in | in / on; What colour is it? It's red / green / yellow. | |
| 9 | n | **nine**, nest, nut | How old are you? I am … years old. | |
| 10 | o | **orange**, octopus, ostrich | triangle, circle, square; red, orange; Yes / no. It's a (red) square. Please give me a (red) (square). | on, in, it, sit, hit |
| 11 | p | **paint**, pig, parrot | pink, purple; person, people I can eat / swim / paint / drink / read / jump / sleep. His name is…; Her name is… | |
| 12 | y & g | **yellow**, yo-yo, yoghurt **girl**, green, grapes, goat | big, little; up, down, around; girl, boy, man, woman It is (little and red). What is it? | |
| 13 | e & u | **elephant**, egg, elbow **umbrella**, under, up | on, in, under, up, down, around The (elephant) is (on / in / under) the box. | ten, net, nest, nut, sun, up, *Short vowels*: hat, hot, hit, hut; pan, pen, pin; man, men, etc… |

| Lesson | Letter | Character's words (Keyword in **bold**) | Topics / speaking vocabulary | Word-building (phonics) |
|---|---|---|---|---|
| 14 | **k & q** | **king**, **queen** kangaroo, key, kite quilt, question, quill | Who is…? Who has…? | |
| 15 | **f & r** | **fire**, fish, flowers **ring**, red, rocket | Favourite foods: I like… Who am I? (rice, cake, ice-cream, milk, eggs, yoghurt, sandwiches, nuts, grapes, fruit) | sun, run, fun red, Fred |
| 16 | **l & v** | **lamp**, lighthouse, leg **vase**, vegetables, van | Rooms: bedroom, living room, kitchen, bathroom; Verbs: (review) | |
| 17 | **j & b** | **jacket**, jigsaw, juice **ball**, bed, blue | Animals: It's a (…) (cat, dog, horse, monkey, tiger, snake, octopus, elephant, duck) | bed, red |
| 18 | **w & x** | **water**, window, web **box**, fox, six | Who is wearing (…)? (shirt, dress, trousers, shoes) | wet, six |
| 19 | **z** | **zebra**, zero, zoo | review animals | *Review all medial vowels* |
| 20 | **sh** | **ship**, shell, fish, splash | | ship, shell, shop |
| 21 | **ch** | **chin**, **children**, chick, bench | | chin, chick, children |

plus a continuously expanding vocabulary, as described on page 10.

# The teaching order

**c**, **a**, **d**, **h**, **m**, **t**, **s**, **i**, **n**, **o**, **p**, **y&g**, **e&u**, **k&q**, **f&r**, **l&v**, **j&b**, **w&x**, **z**, **sh**, **ch**

Reasons for the teaching order:

★ Avoids confusion by keeping similarly shaped letters (like **b** and **d**) far apart.

★ Children can build more words more quickly when they learn letters in this order. (First words: **dad**, **cat**, **hat**, **mat**, **cats**, **sad**…)

★ From Lesson 12, we introduce two letters per lesson so that you can cover the whole alphabet AND a basic listening and speaking vocabulary within a relatively short period.

# What language will children learn?

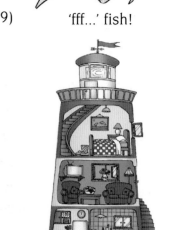

'fff...' fish!

## Direct teaching (See Scope and Sequence Chart pages 8 and 9)

**Characters' words:** Children learn the **a-z** letter sounds (plus **sh** and **ch**) and three words beginning with each of these sounds. This strand also develops children's listening skills. The ability to listen for and identify sounds in a word is an important first reading skill.

**Topics:** In each lesson there is also a vocabulary strand grouped by topic. Topics covered in this programme include: colours, **numbers, foods, parts of the body, shapes, rooms,** verbs, and family . Children use these words in songs, activities and games.

**Sentences**: Children hear and use simple sentences in a variety of listening and speaking activities in the *Student Book*, the *Workbook* and the *Activity Bank* (pages 84-88).

**Word-building:** There are optional word-building activities spread throughout the Lesson Plans. Children learn playful strategies for blending and segmenting regular words. (See the last column on pages 8 and 9.)

## Indirect teaching

**Listening vocabulary:** The structure and instruction language of the Lesson Plans is deliberately consistent, allowing pupils and teachers to become familiar with recurring activities and language.

Simple sentences are scripted into the Lesson Plans in the form of questions, instructions, songs and statements that children hear in every lesson. Try to demonstrate the meanings with actions. At first, the children may not understand or use these sentences, but hearing them in every lesson will soon make them part of their expanding vocabulary.

**'Real-life' situations:** Children will also pick up any other vocabulary you choose to use consistently in your classroom, for example;
"Stand up." "Please open your books." "Write your name here."

# What is our approach to teaching English?

## Methodology

Letterland ELT…

★ integrates **language** teaching with teaching **letter sounds**, using Letterland's unique 'pictogram approach'

★ is thoroughly **multi-sensory**

★ uses **direct** teaching and **indirect** teaching so that children are exposed to a carefully controlled set of vocabulary and structures

★ is highly **interactive** and includes group work and pair work as well as individual activities

★ provides a highly **motivating learning environment**

## The pictogram approach to ELT

At the heart of Letterland teaching are carefully designed pictogram mnemonics. Each Letterland pictogram combines a plain letter shape with a familiar character whose name begins with that letter's sound (Annie Apple, ă …; Firefighter Fred, 'fff…'). These 'audio-visual' images help children to 'see' a letter's sound.

Letterland pictograms radically accelerate the pace at which children 'crack the code' of English, beginning with one of the first skills children need to become successful readers of English - the ability to listen for and identify **a-z** sounds at the beginning of spoken words (phonemic awareness).

ESL teachers have found that the emotional appeal of these characters also creates the ideal conditions for learning and remembering a new *language*. The imaginative, alternative reality of 'Letterland' stimulates children's natural curiosity and motivates them to learn more about each of their Letterland friends.

Children enjoy imitating what the characters say and do. This imitative aspect recreates the interest and motivation we feel when we acquire our native language.

# Main components

## Big Picture Code Cards

48 double-sided full colour cards feature the **a-z** Letterland pictogram characters. Use the picture side to introduce each new Letterlander, and the plain side to introduce the letter sound: **Annie Apple, 'ă...'**

Also useful for Quick Dash revision, role-play, Live Spelling and finger-tracing.

Annie Apple       'ă...'

## Vocabulary Cards

78 picture cards feature three pictures for each **a-z** letter sound. Use these cards to present each character's alliterative words, and for whole-class review activities.

The large picture-coded words on the backs of the cards help develop phonemic awareness of initial sounds. The corners feature rhyming words.

## Student Book & CD*

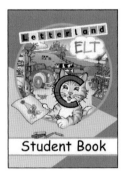

Student Book

There are four *Student Book* pages per lesson. The *Student Book* activities consolidate and review language and letter sounds that are first presented using oral activities set out in the *Teacher's Guide*. Instructions for using each page in the *Student Book* are in the *Student Book* CD Booklet.

Also useful for at-home revision.

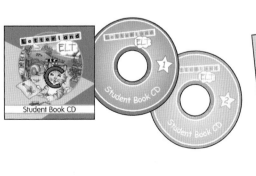

*CD includes Alphabet Songs as part of each lesson.*

## Workbook

There are two *Workbook* pages per lesson:
The first page reviews the target sound, previous letter sounds and alliterative words.

The second page consolidates new topic-based vocabulary and usually includes a simple speaking activity or game, which children can complete in pairs or on their own.

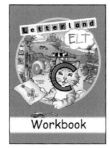
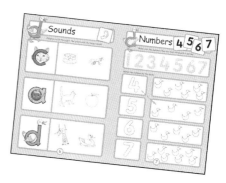

## Handwriting Book

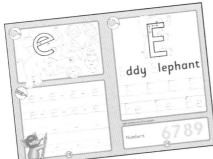

There are two pages per letter. The first page contains a finger tracing activity and a writing practice activity for lower case letters.
The second page contains uppercase and lower case letters plus numbers 1-10.

# Highly recommended

## Letterland Alphabet Frieze

Excellent interactive teaching tool for finger-tracing and letter spotting. A great reference point for the whole class.

## ELT Alphabet Songs CD

Teaches the ELT *Alphabet Songs* in alphabetical order. Useful for continuous play in the classroom, for presentations and for at-home revision.

Note: These songs and the Letterland theme song (page 17) are also featured on the ELT *Student Book* CD, in the Letterland ELT Teaching order.

## Activity Books:

Use these Activity Books as a fun way to follow up your **a-z**, **sh** and **ch** teaching – this time in alphabetical order. (For use at school or at home.)

See page 75 for details of each book.

## Letterland ABC

26 scenes showing each of the **a-z** Letterland characters surrounded by objects beginning with the target sound. A great resource to introduce children to the magical land of letters.

## Alphabet Adventures

Another fantastic picture book to help to introduce the concept of Letterland being a special place to visit.

## Action Tricks Poster

Do the actions, make the sounds and learn the alphabet. The actions help to develop multi-sensory memory cues for letter sounds. Actions form part of each lesson plan so this poster provides a great focal point and reminder for the whole class.

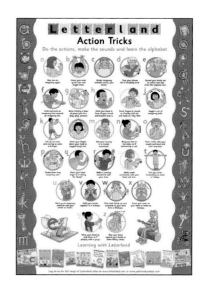

## Monkey Hand Puppet

Monkey is an optional resource for those of you who enjoy using puppets. Use Monkey to help you present the keyword in each lesson.

# ★★★ Chapter 2 ★★★

## Training

## Where is Letterland?

How will you communicate the idea of a secret, special place called Letterland to your children in the very first lesson?

Using picture books such as *Alphabet Adventures* or the *Letterland ABC* will allow children to see the characters in Letterland and get a sense of the magical world of letters.

If you do speak the children's home language you can tell them:

**Letterland is the place where all the letters live. When most people look in a book, all they can see is plain black letters. That's because they don't know about Letterland and they haven't met the Letterland characters yet.**

**In Letterland you can *see* the characters and they help you remember the shape and sound of each letter.**

# ✓ PART 1: How to use the Lesson Plans...

## Section 1: Keyword Routine

A fun and familiar way to begin each lesson is to present the keyword with the 'What's in the box?' song. If possible, use a real object or toy to represent the keyword*. Otherwise use a *Vocabulary Card*.

### What is the keyword?

Begin each lesson by presenting a simple word that begins with the target sound. Whenever possible, the keyword is part of the character's name (**cat** is the keyword for Clever Cat's lesson), so that when you introduce a new Letterlander, children can link his or her name to a word they have learned first.

If you enjoy using puppets, the *Monkey Hand Puppet* can help you present the keyword, and to act as a guide through Letterland.

### Presenting the keyword: What's in the box???

Decorate a big box for your classroom. Before the children come in, put the keyword object or *Vocabulary Card* in the box. Start each lesson by asking: **What's in the box today?** Then sing the 'What's in the box?' Song (on the *Student Book* CD.)

### Questions and answers

You can also use this introductory session to teach and practise useful structures. For example:

> **What's your name?**
> **What's in the box today?**
> **What is it? What is it?**
> **It's a cat! It's a .....!**

Ask children to repeat the keyword. Check understanding by pointing to other objects and people: **Is this a cat? Is that a cat? Is she a cat? Is he a cat? What colour is this cat? Do you like cats? Point to the cat's ears.** etc...

*For a list of the keyword objects or *Vocabulary Cards* you need to collect, see pages 8 and 9.

# Section 2: Meet the character and learn the letter sound

## Character name

To introduce the new character, invite a child to find the character on the *Alphabet Frieze* or from a selection of *Big Picture Code Cards*.

Say the character name together a few times.

## Theme Song: Go to Letterland

If time allows, sing the Letterland Song (on the ELT *Student Book* CD and ELT *Alphabet Songs* CD) and make a pretend journey to Letterland.

The children could all hold hands and pretend to jump into a giant book. Let the children decide whether to pretend to climb onto a magic carpet and fly to Letterland or simply close their eyes for a few moments and then open them to arrive in Letterland.

## The Sounds Trick

Use the *Picture Code Card* and the character' special 'Sounds Trick', to help children learn their letter sounds:

**To discover my letter sound, just START to say my name:** Clever Cat, 'c...'

Whenever you talk about letter sounds, always turn to the PLAIN LETTER side of your *Big Picture Code Card*. Use the picture-side only to talk about the character's Letterland name. This will ensure that children learn the important skill of linking the plain letter shape to the letter sound.

*Note*: The Sounds Trick will help children learn each letter's **regular** sound. For changes in sound, see page 32: Dealing with exceptions.

## Abbreviations

Occasionally you will find character names abbreviated in the Lesson Plans, for example, 'Clever Cat' is written as 'CC' or Harry Hat Man as 'HHM'.When talking to students, characters should always be given their full names. This abbreviation is simply to reduce repetition within the *Teacher's Guide*.

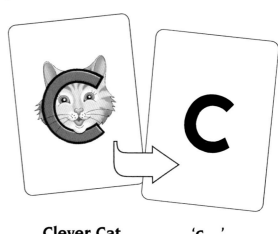

**Clever Cat**           'c...'

## The Actions Trick

Each Letterland character has an 'Action Trick' to help remember its letter sound. Teach the children to say the letter sound when they make the action. (Use your *Action Tricks Poster* or see pages 82-83 for an illustration of each action, and some activity ideas).

'ĕ...'

'mmm...'

## The ELT Alphabet Songs

You will find the songs on the ELT *Student Book* CD and on the ELT *Alphabet Songs* CD.

Annie Apple's Alphabet Song

Annie Apple, she says 'a...', she says 'a...', she says 'a...'.

Annie Apple, she says 'a...'.

a...a...a

a...a...a

When you sing the song together, show the picture-side of the *Big Picture Code Card* each time you sing the character name. Turn to the plain letter side each time you make the sound. Children can also make the character's action each time they make the letter sound.

You could also write up the lyrics to use as a shared reading text. This will strengthen the letter shape / sound link, give practice in reading the character names, and the common words, **she**, **he** and **says**.

## Picture-coding

To picture-code a letter, children add the Letterlander's picture details to a plain black letter. Picture-coding helps children to make the letters their own and it greatly increases their attention to the shape, sound and direction of each letter.

For the first few lessons, you may like to provide large plain black letters for children to picture-code. When they are ready, children can draw their own plain letters and then picture-code them.

There will be many opportunities to use vocabulary relating to colours and parts of the body. For example: **First draw Clever Cat's ears. Draw Annie Apple's eyes, nose and mouth. What colour is Annie Apple? What colour is Harry Hat Man's hat?** and so on.

dog

cat

You can also use picture-coding to draw attention to target sounds in words. You don't have to be an artist – simply 'hand-code' the letters by adding stick figures or simple details to the letters.

## Quick Dash

Once you have introduced four or five letters, use this section of the lesson to review all previous letter sounds by using the 'Quick Dash' routine:

★ Hold up each *Big Picture Code Card* in turn. Show the picture-coded side and ask for the character name. Quickly turn the card over and ask for the letter sound only.

★ Next do a dash through the plain letters and ask children to give you the letter sounds only. Increase the pace as children become more familiar with the routine, aiming for a Quick Dash through all the letter sounds.

★ If you are teaching traditional letter names (ay, bee, see, dee…etc.) you could add a third question: **What is his / her letter name?**

★ For a more detailed discussion of when to introduce letter names, see page 31.

| TEACHER | CHILDREN |
|---|---|
| 1) Who is this? | Clever Cat |
| 2) What sound does she make? | 'c…' |
| | |
| 1) And who is this? | Annie Apple |
| 2) What sound does she make? | 'ă …' |

Clever Cat            'c…'

Annie Apple            'ă…'

## Assessment outcome:
## Say the letter sounds in response to the plain letters

If you would like to measure and record your pupil's knowledge of letter sounds in a more formal way, use *Pupil Record Sheet* 1 (page 89) along with the following activity:

★ Write 6 plain letters on a piece of paper (for example: **c**, **a**, **d**, **h**, **m**, **t**).

★ Ask a child to say each letter sound as you point to it.

For best results, wait at least a week after the children have learnt the last letter in the group, and build in lots of review activities into your lessons, such as the Quick Dash (above), the Letter line (page 25) or other review activities in the Activity Bank (pages 84-88).

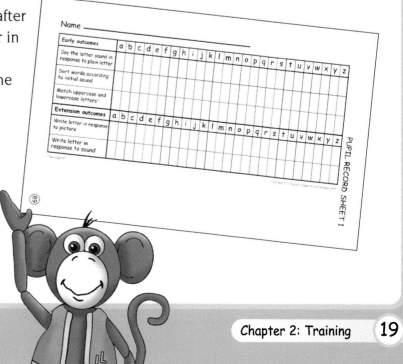

# Section 3: The Character's words

First present the three new alliterative words using *Vocabulary Cards*. Then the children use these new words in simple speaking activities. Finally, consolidate the new letter sounds and vocabulary using the ELT *Student Book* & CD.

## Present the Character's words

Use the *Vocabulary Cards* to introduce the three words that begin with each Letterlander's sound (e.g. 'Clever Cat's words' are **cat**, **car** and **cake**). Show the picture side first and say the word. Then turn over the card and emphasise the target sound as you say the word again: cake, c..., cake

Next, use the word in a simple sentence of your own that links the word to the Letterland character, e.g.

Clever Cat likes cake. Clever Cat has a red car.  Clever Cat is a cat. Harry Hat Man has a green hat. Harry Hat Man has a green house. Harry Hat Man has a horse. Is it green? No! And so on.

## Use the new words (More advanced)

The Activity Bank (pages 84-88) contains simple, fun activities for using the new alliterative vocabulary. In each game, the words in bold are structures that children will need to understand and / or say in order to play the game, for example: **What is it? Is this a...? / Who likes...? / What's missing? / Where's the...? / I like (cake). Who am I?** etc.

You can play each game as a whole-class activity using *Big Picture Code Cards* and *Vocabulary Cards*. Children can also play these games in pairs, using the smaller, photocopiable *Student Cards* on pages 91-95.

Choose one or two activities, as time allows.

What is it?

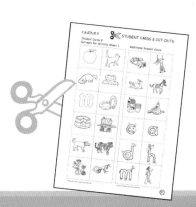

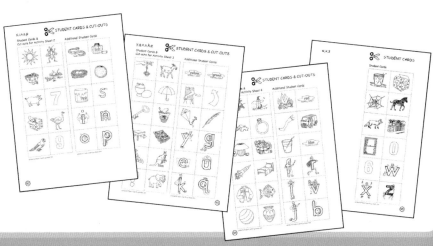

## Student Book & CD activities

Use the first two-page section of each ELT *Student Book* lesson to consolidate the new letter sound and new alliterative words. The first page has a CD component; the 'Find' activity on the second page does not.

From Lesson 12 onwards the book covers two letters per lesson; there are no 'Find' activities in these later lessons.

Instructions for how to use each page in the ELT *Student Book* can be found in the ELT *Student Book* CD *Booklet*. The first page for each letter is always the same, for example:

**1** Children first listen, then say Clever Cat's letter sound with the CD.

**3** Children say Clever Cat's three words with the CD, pointing first at the picture, then at the initial letter and finally they run their fingers under the whole word as they say:
**cat, 'c...', cat**

**2** Children finger trace Clever Cat's letter as they say her sound again with the CD.

**4** Children point to Clever Cat's letter each time they hear her sound on her ELT *Alphabet Song*.

You may wish to teach this additional vocabulary. (See the *Student Book* CD *Booklet* for details.)

The Vowel Man (long vowel character) is included in each of the five vowel lessons. Introduce the Vowel Man, his letter name and his Action Trick. (See also page 31.)

## Section 4: Letter shapes

Each Letterlander has a lower case and a capital letter shape, and both their letter shapes make the same sound in words.

### Reading Direction

Display a Reading Direction sign in your room. You will notice that most of the characters like to face, look or move in the Reading Direction (from left to right). The Reading Direction concept helps children to picture-code and form letters correctly. It also helps to avoid common reversals (for example **b** / **d** and **p** / **q**).

## Reading Direction

The exceptions are Golden Girl, Quarrelsome Queen and Zig Zag Zebra. Golden Girl gets giddy if she faces the Reading Direction while she is on her swing, the queen is far too quarrelsome to face the Reading Direction and Zig Zag Zebra is too shy!

### Find the letter

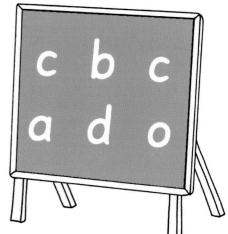

Write some lower case letters on the board, including the target letter. Choose a child to find the target letter. **Can you find Dippy Duck's letter?** Also include some previously taught letters and use the opportunity to review these letter shapes and sounds as well. **Can you find Annie Apple's letter? What is her sound?**

### Form the letter

Draw a huge letter on the board and picture-code it by adding simple picture details. Use the large letter (or a *Big Picture Code Card*) to demonstrate the correct stroke sequence.

**Air trace** Next, create the letter shape in the air. Make sure you ALL face the board as you model the correct stroke (teacher included). If you face the children, they will see you making the letter backwards!

Air-tracing helps provide each child with a physical memory pattern for the correct sequence of strokes. You will also be able to see at a glance who is having difficulty making the correct shape.

In each Lesson Plan we have suggested a simple phrase to help children relate the starting point to a part of the body or to another simple word. For example: **Start at Clever Cat's ear. Start at Annie Apple's leaf. Start at Dippy Duck's back.**

## Capital letter stories

In Letterland, there is always a story to explain changes in shape or sound. You can introduce the new capital letter shape using the *Letterland Alphabet Frieze*, *Capital Big Picture Code Cards* or the *Character Name Flashcards* (page 105) before children move on to the handwriting activities in the ELT *Handwriting Book*. To help children link a lower case letter to its capital letter shape, there are brief capital letter stories (details in each Lesson Plan). If you don't speak the children's home language remember you can demonstrate by miming!

I'm so happy to start a sentence or a name that I do a handstand with my hat on!

## Handwriting Book activities

The ELT *Handwriting Book* contains
2 pages per letter.

**1** Finger-tracing the hollow letters
prepares children for writing
letters correctly.

**2** This activity gives children
lots of opportunities to
make the correct lower
case letter shape.

**3** To help children recognise the 26 character
names as sight words, explain that each
Letterlander usually appears TWICE in his
or her own name!

**4** Children learn the relative sizes of the upper
and lower case letters by writing them in
pairs.

**5** Children learn to write numbers 1-10.

## Assessment outcome:
## Write letters in response to a sound

If you would like to measure and record your
pupils' ability to write letters independently use
*Pupil Record Sheet* 1 (page 89) along with the
following activity:

★ Call out 6 letter sounds, one by one. Ask:
**How can we write this sound?**

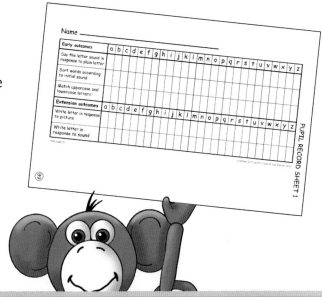

# Section 5: Phonemic awareness & phonics

First, children identify and isolate the first sound in words. Then they use these words in a simple speaking activity. In some lessons, there are also optional word-building activities. The activities grow to include each new letter that you teach, so revision is built into each lesson.

# Phonemic awareness...

Phonemic awareness is the ability to hear, identify and manipulate the individual sounds (phonemes) in spoken words. It is now widely accepted that phonemic awareness is a crucial first step in learning to read for both first and second language learners. If children can hear and isolate individual sounds in spoken words, they can make quick progress in phonics (linking phonemes to written language).

## Word sort & letter line

Include a cumulative word-sort activity and a letter line at this point in each lesson.

★ Hand out *Big Picture Code Cards* for all the letters you have learnt so far and invite some children to hold (or wear) the cards at the front of the class. (If children wear the cards they can concentrate on holding and displaying the *Vocabulary Cards*.)

★ Hand out all the matching *Vocabulary Cards* to the remaining children.

★ The children holding the *Vocabulary Cards* look at the <u>picture-sides only</u> and decide which Letterlander starts the word on their card. Then they hand the *Vocabulary Card* over to the correct child at the front.

★ Help the children in the 'letter line' (at the front) to role-play the characters and present their words:

I'm Clever Cat. I say 'c..' in words like cat, car and cake.
I'm Annie Apple. I say 'a…' in words like ant, apple and acrobat.
I'm Dippy Duck. I say 'd…' in words like duck, dog and dinosaur.

★ Depending on the age and ability of the children, they could flip the cards over to the word side and invite the rest of the class to repeat the word with them.

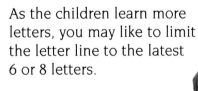

★ As the children learn more letters, you may like to limit the letter line to the latest 6 or 8 letters.

## Presenting a-z

A great way to complete your **a-z** lessons is to present the whole alphabet, (in alphabetical order), using the letter line (left). The children could share their routine with another class, at assembly, or at a parent evening.

## Assessment outcome:
## Sort words according to initial sound

If you would like to formally assess and record students' phonemic awareness of initial sounds, use *Pupil Record Sheet 1* (page 89) along with the photocopiable *Cut-outs and Activity Sheets 1-5* (pages 91–100):

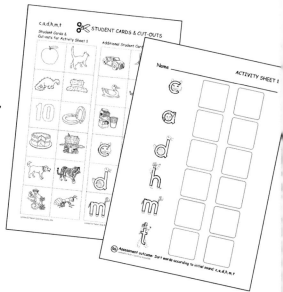

★ On *Activity Sheets 1-4*, children stick pictures next to the Letterlander with the same initial sound.

★ On *Activity Sheet 5*, they circle the objects that begin or end with the target sound.

For best results, do the assessment at least a week after the children have learnt the last letter in each group of 6 letters. Also build lots of review activities into your lessons, such as the 'Word sort & letter line' (page 25) or other 'Review activities' from the Activity Bank (pages 85-86).

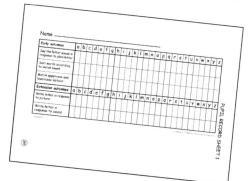

## Assessment outcome:
## Write letter in response to picture

★ For older or more advanced children, (or later on in the year) use *Activity Sheets 6-9* (pages 101-104): Children write the matching initial letter next to each picture.

# Phonics...

Phonics teaches the link between spoken sounds and written language. Ten of the Lesson Plans* contain phonics activities such as 'Live Reading', 'Live Spelling', and 'Spelling Pictures'. These word-building activities are a great way to teach blending (combining letter sounds to form a word) and segmenting (breaking up a word into its individual sounds) in a multi-sensory way.

## Live Reading

During Live Reading sessions, *you* arrange the children in a word at the front of the classroom. Then help them to read it by modelling segmenting and blending. To begin with, use the picture-sides of the *Big Picture Code Cards*.

For example, arrange three 'letter children' in the word **cat**, and stand behind them. Help the class to segment the word **cat** into its individual sounds by pointing to each letter child: **What is Clever Cat's sound? What is Annie Apple's sound? What is Talking Tess's sound?**

Then blend the sounds back together again. Turn the cards over to the plain letter sides and repeat with just the letter sounds (c…a…t) - first by yourself, then with the children. Next, blend the first two sounds together, (ca…t). Finally blend all three sounds to read the whole word (cat). (Note: If children need additional support to begin with, use the picture-coded letters for blending. But move on to the plain letter sides as soon as you can, in order to reinforce the link between the sound and the plain letter shape).

## Live Spelling

During Live Spelling sessions, you 'slow-speak' a word out-loud. Children decide which letters are needed to form that word.

First, hand out *Big Picture Code Cards* for all the words that you want to build in that lesson (**s, r, f, u, n** for **sun, run, fun**).

To help children segment the word into its individual sounds, 'slow-speak' it for them. (Stretch it out, but don't break the word apart, e.g. **sssunnn.**)

The children then repeat the word in 'slow-speak' and try to identify the individual sounds. Those holding the cards decide if their letter is needed to build the word. If so, they come to the front and line up in the correct order. The rest of the class can check the resulting word by blending it as a whole class activity. (See Live Reading, above.)

* Lessons 3, 5, 7, 10, 13, 15, 17, 19, 20 and 21

Most Lesson Plans contain a Live Spelling word chain (e.g. **sun-> run-> fun**), where changing one letter only will result in a new word. After building **sun**, slow-speak the new word (**rrrunnn**) and ask who needs to sit down and who needs to come up to build the new word. The '**r**' child should then come to the front and replace the '**s**' child to make the new word. Do the same with **fun**.

*Note*: After each session it is a good idea to ask children to write and then read the word or words you have built.

## Spelling Pictures

To make a 'Spelling picture', children picture-code each letter in a regular word, and then illustrate the word in the space around it. Later on, they can use their own illustrations to help them re-read the word. Display good examples on a wall, so that they can be shared.

Not all words are suitable for 'Spelling Pictures'. It is best to use concrete words that are easy and enjoyable to illustrate. Some of the 'Spelling Pictures' children could make in this programme include: **cat**, **cats**, **hat**, **hats**, **ten**, **up**, **ducks**, **sun**, **wet**, **six**, **fish** and **children**. (See the Lesson Plans for details.)

You could create a Letterland Spelling and Reading Book for each child (made up of each child's 'Spelling Pictures' and a list of reading vocabulary) for them to take home and share with their parents. You will find a photocopiable cover for the book on page 108. You will also find a list of *Reading Words*, which contains the Live Reading and Live Spelling words featured in the Lesson Plans. Put the cover on the front of each book and the reading list at the back before you bind each child's book together.

# Section 6: Topics

In section 6 of each Lesson Plan, you will find ideas for presenting words that are grouped in the following topics: colours, **numbers**, **foods**, **parts of the body**, **shapes**, **rooms**, verbs, family... and more.

## Teacher's Guide activities

Each lesson has different activities for teaching the new topic-based vocabulary - including songs, movement, chants and games. You will find these new words, together with details of how to teach them in each Lesson Plan.

## Student Book & CD activities

Two pages of each 4-page lesson in the *Student Book* are dedicated to the new topic-based vocabulary. Instructions for using each page of the *Student Book* can be found in the booklet that accompanies the *Student Book* CD.

# Section 7: Review and pair work

In Section 7, children work alone or in pairs as they complete their *Workbook* activities, which include games and simple speaking activities.

## Workbook activities

Each lesson in the *Workbook* has 2 pages. The first page is a letter-sound activity that reviews the target sound, previous sounds and the characters' alliterative words.

The second page consolidates new topic-based vocabulary. Many of these pages feature a simple speaking activity or game, which children can complete in pairs.

Instructions for using each page are included in the *Workbook*.

# ✓ PART 2: General Information

## Teaching the correct letter sounds

THIS IS VERY IMPORTANT!

The key to making quick progress in reading and spelling is to teach the correct letter sounds. For example, the correct sounds for 'c…' and 't…' are whispered sounds. There should be no voice. If you add voice you will get the incorrect sounds 'cuh' and 'tuh'. Incorrect sounds can turn a simple word like **cat** into a meaningless word like 'cuh-a-tuh'.

Incorrect sounds can also lead to spelling mistakes such as **bt** when trying to spell **butter** ('buh', 'tuh').

You can all listen to the correct letter sounds on the *Letterland ELT Alphabet Songs* CD or the *Letterland ELT Student Book* CD. The Letterland Sounds Trick (page 17) gives the usual sound for each **a-z** letter.

You can also use the following three simple categories as guidelines for pronouncing all the consonant sounds accurately. (*Note*: Some sounds are in more than one category.)

| **Whispered sounds** | **Prolonged sounds** | **Almost closed mouth sounds** |
|---|---|---|
| are never spoken with voice ('c…' not 'cuh'). | can be extended (fff…). | Avoid adding too much 'uh' on to the end of the sound by keeping your mouth almost closed: 'b…' not 'bee' or 'buh'; 'd…' and not 'dee' or 'duh'. |
|  |  |  |

# Letter sounds vs letter names

Many children may already be aware of some of the traditional letter names from songs or learning at home, however, they are not much help to a child when it comes to reading and spelling. For example, the letter names 'see, ay, tee' will not help a child to read the word **cat**, because they do notgive the correct letter sounds.

The 21 consonant letter names (bee, see, dee, eff, jee, aitch, etc.) are never used in reading. 15 consonant letter names actually begin with another letter's sound (see, eff, aitch, ell, em, etc…). An added confusion for language learners is the fact that many of the letter names sound like other words, for example, **a**, **I**, **see**, **are**, **tea**, **you** and **why**.

Using the Letterland character names (Annie Apple, Bouncy Ben, Clever Cat, etc.) gives you a temporary alternative to the traditional but confusing alphabet names. Now you can talk about 'Clever Cat's whispered 'c…' sound' and 'Clever Cat's letter shape'.

Once the children have learnt the correct letter sounds you can safely introduce the letter names.

*Note*: If you prefer to introduce the letter names along with the letter sounds, you could introduce a third round of questions in your Quick Dash routine: **What is his / her letter name?** (See page 19.)

# The Vowel Men say their letter names in words

In Letterland, the only characters who say their letter names in words are the five Vowel Men: Mr A the Apron Man; Mr E the Easy Magic Man; Mr I the Ice-cream Man; Mr O the Old Man and Mr U the Uniform Man. All the other characters love to say their *letter sounds* in words. Whenever children role-play a Vowel Man saying his name, the action is the same: they shoot up their right hand and say the letter name with enthusiasm, to let everyone know there is a Vowel Man in the word.

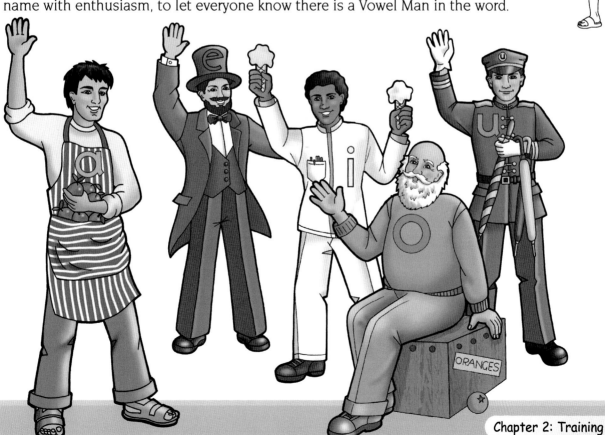

## Dealing with exceptions

To begin with, children will use the Letterland Sounds Trick (page 17) to discover each **a–z** letter's *usual* sound. They will build and read 'regular' words that are made up of these usual sounds. But they will also come across less regular words like: **circle**, **eyes**, **one**, **two**, **three**....where letters are not making their usual sounds.

There are stories in Letterland teaching to explain these changes in sound. However this is part of the more advanced Letterland teaching. At this early stage of ELT teaching a nice way of identifying and making the exception 'safe' is to put a wavy line under the irregular parts.

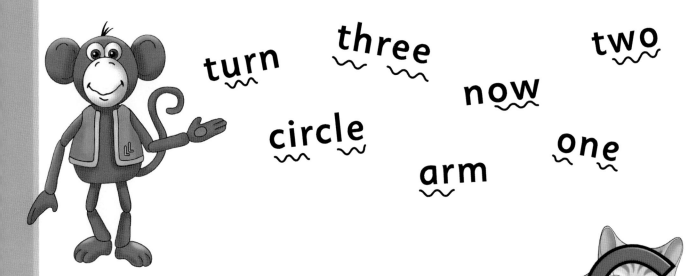

turn    three    two

now

circle    one

arm

## Cross—curricular opportunities

For those of you following a cross-curricular approach, there are many ways to extend your study of letter shapes and sounds into other areas.

colours

★   Relate the characters to other activities that begin with their sound. For example, learn about **c**olours when you meet Clever Cat, and bring attention to her sound at the start of the word. **P**ainting with Peter Puppy, **f**ood with Firefighter Fred, etc.

★   Organise a Letterland Day or Event. For example: an assembly, a Letterland Dressing-up Day, or a Letterland Olympics.

★   Relate Letterland to arts and crafts. For example, make masks or puppets of the characters out of card or papier mâché. Or use modelling dough and make thick letters in one colour and the characters in other colours.

# ★★★ Chapter 3 ★★★

# Lesson Plans

## Timing and flexibility

You may not have time (or want to) complete all the activities in each Lesson Plan. This guide is yours to use flexibly, according to your particular needs. As a rough guide, each Lesson Plan contains material for 90+ minutes. There are 21 Lesson Plans in this chapter.

There are plenty of activities in the Lesson Plans to extend older or more advanced children – feel free to leave them out if your children are not ready. You may, for example, like to postpone even the brief introduction to long vowels, capital letters and word-building for a later stage.

## Assessment outcomes

Here are some of the outcomes you will be able to measure and record if you choose to use the continual assessment activities in the Lesson Plans (see also pages 19, 24, and 26). *Activity Sheets* and *Pupil Record Sheets* are on pages 89-104. All of these outcomes are key steps in learning to read and spell in English.

### Early outcomes:

★   Say letter sound in response to plain letter. (See page 19.)

★   Sort words according to initial sound. (*Activity Sheets* 1-5; see page 26.)

★   Match upper-case and lower-case letters. (See page 87.)

### Extension outcomes for older or more advanced children:

★   Write letter in response to picture. (*Activity Sheets* 6-9; see page 26.)

★   Write letter in response to sound. (See page 24.)

★   Read and spell a selection of regular words. (See page 90.)

Do a round of assessment activities after every 5 or 6 letters.

Tip: For best results, do each assessment at least a week after teaching the 6th letter in each group of 6 letters. Include lots of review activities in your lessons during that week. Suggestions for when to do each assessment are included in the Lesson Plans.

## Preparations

Before you begin your first Letterland lesson, it is a good idea to make the following preparations:

✔ Read Chapter 2: Training (pages 15-32).

✔ Get a CD player.

✔ Collect keyword objects (pages 8-9). Alternatively, use your *Vocabulary Cards*.

✔ Decorate a big box for the 'What's in the box?' routine (page 16). If you do not have your own classroom, try creating a fold-up box!

✔ You may also like to collect additional objects for a Sound Bag. A Sound Bag is simply a collection of small objects that begin with the sounds you plan to teach. You could use these in addition to your *Vocabulary Cards*.

✔ If possible, put up the Alphabet Frieze at an easy finger-tracing height for children. Alternatively, display a selection of *Big Picture Code Cards* before each lesson (including the new Letterlander), so that children can identify the new character in Section 2 of each lesson.

✔ Put up a Reading Direction sign and arrows (page 22) above the space where you plan to build words during Live Spelling (pages 27-28). Any child who reverses letters or normally reads print from right to left will benefit from having a Reading Direction arrow on their desk as well.

✔ *Optional*: You may like to use costumes (page 88) for the role-play activities in Section 6 of each lesson. Parents often enjoy helping out with costumes and props.

✔ You may like to purchase a separate ELT *Alphabet Songs* CD. (These songs are also included on the ELT *Student Book* CD, but do not run consecutively, and follow the Letterland ELT teaching order rather than alphabetical order.)

## Checklist

Here is a checklist to help you prepare for each lesson:

1   Listen to the correct pronunciation of the target sound on the ELT *Student Book* CD.

2   Put the keyword object or *Vocabulary Card* in your decorated box.

3   Have ready all the *Big Picture Code Cards* for all the letters you have learnt so far.

4   Have ready all the *Vocabulary Cards* for all the letters you have learnt so far.

5   Prepare plain black letters for picture-coding.

6   Prepare any photocopiable *Activity Sheets* or *Student Cards* that you may need for the lesson (pages 91-104).

7   Check the 'You will need…' section at the start of the next Lesson Plan for materials that are specific to that lesson.

8   Keep the *Monkey Hand Puppet* out of sight so that the children only see him when he is on your hand and animated at the beginning of each lesson.

# Clever Cat

The stars refer you to more info on how to teach each section!

## Lesson 1

### TEACHING OBJECTIVES:

✔ **c** and **C** letter shapes and sound
✔ Clever Cat's words: cat, car, cake
✔ Extension words: cup, cow, crayons, clown
✔ Oral vocabulary: Hello! I'm (name); one, two three

### YOU'LL NEED:

✔ Picnic mural ② (See below)
✔ List of words ⑤
✔ Number cards: 1-3 ⑥
✔ Also: See the checklist on page 35

## 1 Keyword: cat

See p1(

★ **What's in the box?** Put a toy cat or the **cat** *Vocabulary Card* in the box. Sin 'What's in the box?' on the *Student Book CD One* with the *Monkey Hand Puppe* and follow the Keyword Routine (page 16), **It's a cat!**

## 2 Letter sound

See p17-1

★ **Clever Cat** Can you find a cat on the wall frieze? (or **is this a cat?** Good! This cat lives in Letterland. Her name is Clever Cat.

★ **Theme Song** Sing the 'Letterland Song' and 'go' to Letterland.

★ **Sound** Use the *Big Picture Code Card* and the Letterland Sounds Trick (page 17) to discover Clever Cat's letter sound: **Clever Cat, 'c...'**

★ **Action** Teach CC's Action Trick to help children remember the letter sound.

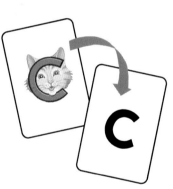
*Action*

★ **Alphabet Song** Sing Clever Cat's ELT *Alphabet Song*. Show the picture-side of the *Card* when you sing her character name. Always turn to the plair letter side when you make her letter sound. Linking the plain letter to the sound is an important preparation for reading.

★ **Picture-code** Children add Clever Cat's picture details to plain black **c**'s Optional: Make a cat's picnic mural and let children stick on thei picture-coded Clever Cat faces. (Template on page 110.)

### Picnic Mural

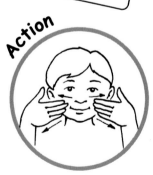

## 3 Clever Cat's words

See p20-

★ **Present** Use *Vocabulary Cards* to introduce the words: **cat**, **car** and **cake**.

★ **Use new words** Choose a few activities from the Activity Bank to giv children an opportunity to use Clever Cat's words. Suggestions: 'Flash Cards' 'What's hiding?' (pages 84-85).

★ **Student Book & CD** Help children to complete the activities on pages 2 and 3 of the ELT *Student Book*. Ideas for using each page in the *Student Book* ar included in the ELT *Student Book CD Booklet*.

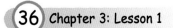

Picture-coding

Clever Cat

**Character Names Trick**
Letterlander's appear TWICE in their capital letter shapes in their own names! This 'trick' will help children to read all the Letterlanders names as sight words.

**Soft 'c'**
Some childrens' names may begin with CC's letter but it may not be making her hard-c sound. See page 32 'Dealing with exceptions.'

## ④ Letter shapes

See p22-24

★ **Find the letter** Write some letters on the board, including a **c**. Ask: **Can you find Clever Cat's letter?** (or **Is this Clever Cat's Letter?**)

★ **Form the letter** Write a big **c** on the board and picture code it. Then air-trace it together, emphasising the starting point at Clever Cat's ear. **Start at Clever Cat's ear.** Repeat with a plain letter and ask the children to imagine Clever Cat's face as they air-trace her letter. **Where is Clever Cat's ear?** Make sure you all face the front when you air-trace, or children will see you making the letter in reverse! (*Optional:* Use Clever Cat's handwriting verse at the back of the ELT *Handwriting Book*.)

★ **Capital letter** Write and picture-code a lower case and capital **c** & **C** on the board. Mime or translate the capital letter story: **Clever Cat has a special trick. She takes a deep breath and gets bigger at the start of names.** Show her *Name Flashcard* (page 105). Notice that Clever Cat's capital letter appears TWICE in her own name.

★ **Handwriting Book** Children complete pages 2 and 3.

## ⑤ Phonemic awareness

See p25-28

★ **Listen & jump!** Have ready a list of words (some start with CC's sound, some do not - you could include the children's names.) Children stand on the outside of a rope circle or mat. Say CC's sound together. Call out one word at a time. If the word starts with CC's sound, children jump into the circle. If the next word does not start with her sound, children jump back out again.

★ **Word sort & letter line** Choose a child to be Clever Cat. Help the child to show CC's three *Vocabulary Cards* and say: **I'm Clever Cat. I say 'c...' in words like cat, car and cake.** See if the children can remember any other 'c...' words, e.g. cup, cow, crayon, clown, etc... (See page 88 for costume ideas.)

★ **Workbook** Children complete page 2 (or save both pages 2 and 3 for a review activity at the end of the lesson.)

## ⑥ Topics

See p29

Numbers

★ **Numbers** Teach numbers **one**, **two** and **three**, using any number cards you may have. Remind children that Clever Cat is very clever and likes to count. **Clever Cat can count to three. One, two, three.** Follow up with an activity using the three number cards. E.g. 'Flash Cards', or 'Order Please' page 84.

★ **Student Book & CD** Help children to complete pages 4 and 5.

## ⑦ Review & pair work

See p29

★ **Workbook** Children complete pages 2 and 3. You might like to do these first *Workbook* pages together as a class. After a few lessons, children can complete the *Workbook* activities in pairs.

# Annie Apple & Mr A
## Lesson 2

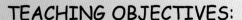

## 1 Keyword: apple

See p16

★ **What's in the box?** Use one **red**, one **green** and one **yellow** apple. Teach these three colours as well as the keyword **apple**. Follow the Keyword Routine. **It's an apple!**

★ **Extension** Play some music and pass the red, yellow and green apples around in a circle. Stop the music and ask: **Who has the red apple? Who has the green apple? What colour is your apple?** etc.

## 2 Letter sound

See p17-1

★ **Annie Apple** **Can you find an apple on the wall frieze? Good! This apple lives in Letterland. Her name is Annie Apple.** If possible, explain that Annie Apple is a talking apple – not an apple for eating!

★ **Theme Song** Go to Letterland!

★ **Sound** Use the Sounds Trick to discover AA's letter sound: **Annie Apple, 'ǎ...**

Action

★ **Action** Children make Annie Apple's sound along with her Action Trick. Review Clever Cat's Action Trick and sound.

★ **Alphabet Song** Sing AA's ELT *Alphabet Song*. Show the picture-side of the Card when you sing her name, and the plain letter when you make her sound.

★ **Picture-code** Children add AA's picture details to a plain black **a**. *Optional* Children add their coded letters to an apple tree mural. (Template on page 110.)

## 3 Annie Apple's words & Mr A

See p20-2

★ **Present** Use *Vocabulary Cards* to introduce: **ant**, **apple** and **acrobat**.

★ **Use new words** Use Annie Apple's words in a game of 'Flash Cards' or 'What's hiding?' (pages 84-85).

★ **Student Book & CD** Pages 6 and 7. Use the Card and the scene on page 7 of the SB to introduce Mr A, the Apron Man (pronounced 'ay'), and explain that Annie Apple belongs to Mr A. Teach his Action Trick (pages 31 and 83).

picture-coding

Annie Apple

## 4 Letter Shapes

See p22-24

★ **Find the letter** Write some letters on the board, including an **a** and a **c**. Can you find Annie Apple's letter? Can you find Clever Cat's letter?

★ **Form the letter** Write a big **a** on the board and picture-code it. Then air-trace it together. Start at Annie Apple's leaf. Repeat with a plain letter. Where is Annie Apple's leaf? (*Optional*: Use AA's handwriting verse.)

★ **Capital letter** Write and picture-code lower case and capital **a** & **A** on the board. Demonstrate or translate the capital letter story: **At the beginning of names, the talking apples sit here on big applestands and say 'ă...'.** Show Annie Apple's *Name Flashcard* (page 105). Notice that her capital letter appears TWICE in her own name. **When Mr A starts an important word, he stands next to the apple stand and says his name, 'A!' (ay).**

★ **Handwriting Book** Pages 4 and 5.

## 5 Phonemic awareness

See p25-28

★ **Word sort & letter line** Choose two children to be Clever Cat and Annie Apple. Then try the role-play activity on page 25, using Clever Cat's and Annie Apple's *Vocabulary Cards*. See if the children know any other 'c...' and 'ă...' words (e.g. cup, cow, clown, crayon; astronaut, apple tree).

★ **Workbook** Page 4 (or save both *Workbook* pages for a review activity at the end of the lesson).

## 6 Topics

See p29

eyes, nose, mouth

★ **Eyes, nose, mouth** Draw a large apple on the board with eyes, nose and mouth. Say each word as you point to Annie Apple's eyes, nose and mouth. Children point to their own faces, repeating the words after you. Then point to your own eyes, nose and mouth, but say the wrong words. Let the children correct you.

★ **Annie Apple says** Touch your eyes / nose / mouth. / Sit down. / Stand up.

★ **Student Book & CD** Help children complete pages 8 and 9. You'll need to prepare numbers for each child to colour in for the Memory Game on page 9 of the *Student Book*. (See *Student Book CD Booklet* page 8.)

## 7 Review & pair work

See p29

★ **Workbook** Pages 4 and 5. If children are ready, let them try to complete the activities in pairs. If not, do them together as a class.

# Dippy Duck

## Lesson 3

See p16
See p17-1
See p20-2

### TEACHING OBJECTIVES:

✔ **d** and **D** letter shapes and sound
✔ Dippy Duck's words: duck, dog, dinosaur
✔ Extension words: draw, daisy, door
✔ Oral vocabulary: four, five, six, seven; mother, father, sister, brother
✔ Word-building: dad

### YOU'LL NEED:

✔ Number cards: Numbers 1-7 ⑥
✔ Chalkboard drawings or pictures: mother, father, sister, brother ⑥
✔ Also: See checklist on page 35

## 1 Keyword: duck

★ **What's in the box?** Use a toy duck or *Vocabulary Card*. Follow the Keyword Routine. **It's a duck!**

## 2 Letter sound

★ **Dippy Duck** Can you find a duck on the wall frieze? Good! This duck lives in Letterland. Her name is Dippy Duck. If possible, explain that Dippy Duck does not sound like other ducks, because she's a Letterland duck.

★ **Theme Song** Go to Letterland!

★ **Sound** Use the *Big Picture Code Card* and the Letterland Sounds Trick to discover Dippy's special sound: **Dippy Duck, 'd...'**

★ **Action** Children make DD's Action Trick along with her sound. Review Clever Cat and Annie Apple's actions and sounds.

**Action**

★ **Alphabet Song** Sing DD's ELT *Alphabet Song*. Show the picture-side of the *Card* when you sing her name and the plain letter side when you make her sound.

★ **Picture-code** Children add DD's picture details to a plain black **d**. *Optional* Children add picture-coded **d**'s to a duckpond mural. (Template on page 110.)

## 3 Dippy Duck's words

**Duckpond Mural**

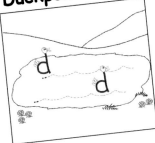

★ **Present** Use *Vocabulary Cards* to introduce the words: **duck**, **dog** and **dinosaur**

★ **Use new words** Choose a few activities from the Activity Bank to give children an opportunity to use the new words. Suggestions: 'What's hiding?' 'Draw and say' (pages 84-85).

★ **Student Book & CD** Pages 10 and 11

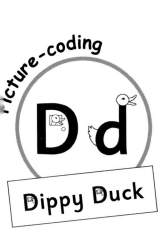

Picture-coding

**D d**

Dippy Duck

Finger puppets

See
p22-24

## ④ Letter shapes

★ **Find the letter** Write some letters on the board, including an **a**, **c** and **d**. *Can you find Annie Apple's letter? Can you find CC's / DD's letter?*

★ **Form the letter** Write a big **d** on the board, picture-code it and air-trace it together. *Start at Dippy Duck's back.* Repeat with a plain letter. *Where is Dippy Duck's back?* Make sure DD ends up facing the Reading Direction! (*Optional*: Use Dippy Duck's handwriting verse, back of ELT *Handwriting Book*.)

★ **Capital letter** Write and picture-code **d** & **D** on the board. Demonstrate or translate the capital letter story: **This is Dippy Duck's duck door. And there she is, saying her sound, 'd…', just inside her door.** Notice that her capital letter appears TWICE in her own name.

★ **Finger puppets** Show children how to find DD's letter shape in their own right hands. Use the templates on page 107. DD loves **d**ancing! The children might enjoy making their little **d**ucks **d**ance to some **d**rums or **d**isco music.

★ **Handwriting Book** Pages 6 and 7.

See
p25-28

## ⑤ Phonemic awareness

★ **Word sort & letter line** Choose three children to be CC, AA and DD. Then try the role-play activity on page 25. See if the children can remember any other 'c…', 'a…' and 'd…' words (cup, carrot, clown, crayon; astronaut, apple-tree; draw, daisy, door). Alternatively, play 'Human Sound Machine' (page 86).

★ **Workbook** Page 6 (or save both *Workbook* pages for the end of the lesson.)

★ **Live Reading** Hand out two DD and one AA *Big Picture Code Card*. Line up the children to create the word **dad**, under your Reading Direction sign. Then help them blend the sounds to read the word. Stand behind the children and ask them to say their sound when you (or Monkey) pats them on the shoulder. Point to the first two quickly, pause, then pat the final one: **da…d**. Then blend the whole word together: **dad**. Draw Dippy Duck's dad on the board to explain the word **dad**, or use the picture on page 12 of the *Student Book*.

Live Spelling

Family

See
p29

## ⑥ Topics

★ **Numbers** Teach numbers **four**, **five**, **six** and **seven**, using number cards. Revise numbers **one**, **two** and **three**. Follow up with a chant or an oral activity using numbers 1-7. (E.g. 'Flash Cards', or 'What's missing?' pages 84-85.)

★ **Family** Make chalkboard drawings of different ducks, or use pictures to pre-teach the words **mother**, **father**, **sister** and **brother**.

★ **Student Book & CD** Page 12 (children blend the word **dad** on paper) and page 13 (numbers 4, 5, 6 & 7).

See
p29

## ⑦ Review & pair work

★ **Workbook** Pages 6 and 7. Children could attempt the counting exercise on page 7 in pairs.

# Harry Hat Man

## TEACHING OBJECTIVES:

✔ **h** and **H** letter shapes and sound
✔ Harry Hat Man's words: hat, house, horse
✔ Extension words: helicopter, hedgehog, hippo
✔ Oral vocabulary: eight, nine; This is a / my... These are my... hand, hand; foot, feet; he, his

## YOU'LL NEED:

✔ Nine hats ①
✔ Number cards: 1-9 ①
✔ Also: See checklist on page 35

### ① Keyword: hat

See p16

★ **What's in the box?** Try to get 9 hats so you can review numbers 1-7, and teach new numbers **eight** and **nine** (as well as the keyword **hat**). It's a hat. This is a hat. These are hats. One, two, three, four, five, six, seven, eight, nine!

### ② Letter sound

See p17-1

★ **Harry Hat Man** Can you find a green hat on the wall frieze? Good! This is Harry Hat Man. Harry Hat Man lives in Letterland. Harry Hat Man doesn't like noise. In fact, he **h**ates noise. Even the sound of his own footsteps gives him a **h**orrible **h**eadache. That's why he never wears shoes, and why he only whispers his 'hhh...' sound in words. Always talk quietly about the Hat Man to make the point!

★ **Theme Song** Go to Letterland!

★ **Sounds Trick** Harry Hat Man, 'hhh...'

★ **Review** Do a 'Quick Dash' (page 19) through all the letter sounds you have taught so far.

*Action*

★ **Action** Learn Harry Hat Man's Action Trick.

★ **Alphabet Song** (See previous Lesson Plan.)

★ **Picture-code** Children add Harry Hat Man's picture details to a plain black **h**.

### ③ Harry Hat Man's words

See p20-2

★ **Present** Use *Vocabulary Cards* to introduce the words: **hat**, **horse** and **house**.

★ **Use new words** Use the new words in a game of 'All in a row' (page 84).

★ **Student Book & CD** Pages 14 and 15

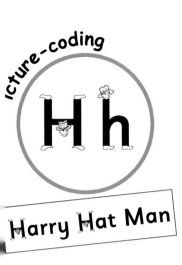

picture-coding

Harry Hat Man

## ④ Letter shapes

See p22-24

★ **Find the letter** Write some letters on the board, including a few previously taught letters and an **h**. Can you find Harry Hat Man's letter? etc...

★ **Form the letter** Write a big **h** on the board, picture-code it and air-trace it together. Start at Harry Hat Man's head. Repeat with a plain letter. Where is Harry Hat Man's head? Make sure he can hop off in the Reading Direction! (*Optional*: Use Harry Hat Man's handwriting verse.)

★ **Capital letter** Write and picture-code lower case and capital **h** & **H** on the board. Demonstrate or translate the capital letter story: When Harry Hat Man can do something so important as start someone's name, he is so happy that he does a handstand. And he even keeps his hat on! Notice that his capital letter appears TWICE in his own name.

★ **Handwriting Book** Pages 8 and 9

## ⑤ Phonemic awareness

See p25-28

★ **Word sort & letter line** Choose four children to be Clever Cat, Annie Apple, Dippy Duck and Harry Hat Man. Then try the role-play activity on page 25, using the *Vocabulary Cards*. See if the children know any other words that start with the target sounds. Or, play 'Knock, knock' (page 86).

★ **Workbook** Page 8 (or save both *Workbook* pages for a review activity at the end of the lesson.)

## ⑥ Topics

See p29

hands and feet

★ **Numbers** Review numbers **1-9** using number cards. Follow up with an oral activity using the number cards (e.g. 'What's missing?' or 'Order Please!' pages 84-85).

★ **This is / these are...** Teach the phrases: This is my hand. / These are my hands. / This is my foot. / These are my feet. - in preparation for the *Student Book* activities and song.

★ **Student Book & CD** Pages 16 and 17

## ⑦ Review & pair work

See p29

★ **Workbook** Pages 8 and 9. Children could attempt the counting exercises on page 9 in pairs.

# Munching Mike
## Lesson 5
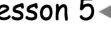

**TEACHING OBJECTIVES:**

✔ **m** and **M** letter shapes and sound
✔ Munching Mike's words: magnet, milk, monkey
✔ Extension words: mouse, mushroom, marshmallows, mango
✔ Oral vocabulary: I'm hungry. Eat. I'm thirsty. Drink. How many...?

**YOU'LL NEED:**

✔ Magnet ①
✔ Number cards: 1-9 ⑥
✔ Sets of objects to count ⑥
✔ Also: See checklist on page 35

## ① Keyword: magnet

See p16

★ **What's in the box?** Try to get a real magnet. **It's a magnet!** If you spea the children's native language, explain that they will be meeting a meta monster who likes to eat metal things, like magnets and motorbikes. Tr picking up various metal and wooden objects. Sort the objects into twc groups. **This is metal.**

## ② Letter sound

See p17-1

**Action**

★ **Munching Mike** **This is Munching Mike. Munching Mike lives in Letterland. He is made of metal.**

★ **Theme Song** Go to Letterland!

★ **Sound** Use the *Big Picture Code Card* and the Sounds Trick to discover Munching Mike's letter sound: **Munching Mike, 'mmm...'**

★ **Action** Teach Munching Mike's Action Trick.

★ **Review** Do a 'Quick Dash' (page 19) through all the letter sounds anc actions you have learnt so far.

★ **Alphabet Song** Sing MM's ELT *Alphabet Song*. Show the picture-side of his *Card* when you sing his name and the plain letter side when you make his sound.

★ **Picture-code** Children add Munching Mike's picture details to a plain black **m**

## ③ Munching Mike's words

See p20-2

★ **Present** Use *Vocabulary Cards* to introduce: **magnet**, **milk** and **monkey**.

★ **Use new words** Choose an activity from the Activity Bank to give childrer an opportunity to use the new words. Suggestion: 'Guess the word' (page 84)

★ **Student Book & CD** Pages 18 and 19

**picture-coding**

**Mm**

**Munching Mike**

See p22-24

## ④ Letter shapes

★ **Find the letter** Write some letters on the board, including a few previously taught letters and an **m**. *Can you find Munching Mike's letter?* etc...

★ **Form the letter** Write a big **m** on the board, picture-code it and air-trace it together. *Start at Munching Mike's tail.* Repeat with a plain letter. *Where is Munching Mike's tail?* Make sure he can move along in the Reading Direction! (*Optional*: Use Munching Mike's handwriting verse.)

★ **Capital letter** Write and picture-code lower case and capital **m** & **M** on the board. Demonstrate or translate the capital letter story: *Munching Mike may look big, but he's really only a little monster (too little to start important words). So his much bigger mum does it for him.* Notice that his capital letter appears TWICE in his own name.

★ **Handwriting Book** Pages 10 and 11

## ⑤ Phonemic awareness

See p25-28

★ **Word sort & letter line** Choose five children to be Clever Cat, Annie Apple, Dippy Duck, Harry Hat Man and Munching Mike. Then try the role-play activity on page 25. See if the children know any other words with the target sounds. Alternatively, choose another Revision game from the Activity Bank (pages 84-88).

★ **Workbook** Page 10 (or save both *Workbook* pages for a review activity at the end of the lesson.)

**I'm hungry!**

## ⑥ Topics

See p29

★ **I'm hungry...** To prepare for Munching Mike's *Student Book* activities, teach the sentences: *I'm hungry. Eat. I'm thirsty. Drink.* Teach an action to go with each verb. (See *Student Book*, page 20 for actions.)

★ **How many...?** Revise the numbers **1-9**. Count sets of objects or chalkboard drawings together, to prepare for the ELT *Student Book* activity on page 19. Use the phrase: *How many...?*

★ **Student Book & CD** Pages 20 and 21

## ⑦ Review & pair work

See p29

★ **Workbook** Pages 10 and 11. Children could attempt the counting exercises on page 11 in pairs.

# Talking Tess

## Lesson 6

### TEACHING OBJECTIVES:

✔ **t** and **T** letter shapes and sound
✔ Talking Tess's words: tiger, telephone, ten
✔ Extension words: two, turtle/tortoise, teddy bear, tree
✔ Oral vocabulary: ten; 1-10; How many fingers…?
✔ Word-building: cat, hat, ham
✔ Spelling pictures: cat, hat

### YOU'LL NEED:

✔ Paper Spelling pictures: cat, hat ⑤
✔ Number cards 1-10 ⑥
✔ Also: See checklist on page 35

## 1 Keyword: telephone

See p16

★ **What's in the box?** Use a real telephone. **It's a telephone!** If possible make it ring in the box! **It's Talking Tess!** Ask the children to say: **Hell**  **Talking Tess.** Have a brief chat then let them say: **Goodbye Talking Tess**

## 2 Letter sound

See p17-1

★ **Talking Tess** **Can you find a telephone on the wall frieze? Good! This is Talking Tess. Talking Tess lives in Letterland.**

★ **Theme Song** Go to Letterland!

★ **Sound** Use the *Big Picture Code Card* and the Sounds Trick: **Talking Tess** **'t…'**

★ **Action** Teach Talking Tess's Actions Trick.

★ **Review** Do a 'Quick Dash' (page 19) through all the letter sounds and actions you have learnt so far.

★ **Alphabet Song** Sing TT's ELT *Alphabet Song*. Show the picture-side of her *Car* when you sing her name and the plain letter side when you whisper her sound

★ **Picture-code** Children add TT's picture details to a plain black **t**.

★ **Assessment** You have now introduced 6 letter sounds. You may like to plan to assess these 6 letter sounds <u>one week from now</u>. *Say the letter soun in response to the plain letters*: c,a,d,h,m,t. (See page 19.)

★ **Present** Use *Vocabulary Cards* to introduce: **telephone**, **tiger**, **ten**.

## 3 Talking Tess's words

See p20-2

★ **Use new words** Choose an activity from the Activity Bank to give childrer an opportunity to use the new words. Suggestion: 'Pass the cards' (page 84)

★ **Student Book & CD** Pages 22 and 23

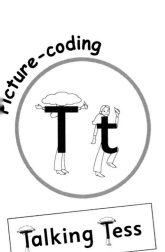

**Picture-coding**

**Talking Tess**

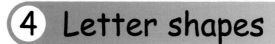

## (4) Letter shapes

See p22-24

★ **Find the letter** Can you find Talking Tess's letter?

★ **Form the letter** Write a big **t** on the board, picture-code it and air-trace it together. Start at her head. Go down to her feet. Then add her arms. Repeat with a plain letter. (*Optional*: Use Talking Tess's handwriting verse.)

★ **Capital letter** Write and picture-code lower case and capital **t** & **T** on the board. Demonstrate or translate the capital letter story: **When TT starts a name, she takes a deep breath and grows so tall that her head disappears in the clouds. We know it's still Tess, because we can still see her arms.** Notice that her capital letter appears TWICE in her own name.

★ **Handwriting Book** Pages 12 and 13.

★ **Assessment** You have now taught 6 letter shapes. Plan to assess them <u>one week from now</u>. *Write letter in response to a sound*: c,a,d,h,m,t. (See page 24).

**Live Reading**

## (5) Phonemic awareness & phonics

See p25-28

★ **Word sort & letter line** Try the role-play activity on page 25.

★ **Workbook** Page 12

★ **Live Reading** Hand out CC, AA, HHM and TT *Big Picture Code Cards*. Line up the children under the Reading Direction sign, to create the word **cat**. Then help the class to blend the sounds to read the word. Stand behind the letter children and ask the seated children to say each sound when you point to it. Point to the first two quickly, pause, then point to the final sound: ca...t. Then blend the whole word: **cat.** Exchange CC for HHM and repeat: Ha...t, hat.

**Live Spelling**

★ *Extension*: **Live Spelling** Take in the cards and hand out CC, AA, TT, HHM and MM B*ig Picture Code Cards*. 'Slow-speak' the word **ham** (hhhammm) and ask the letter children to line up in the correct order to build the word. Then slow-speak the word **hat** and ask which child at the front needs to be replaced to build **hat**. Repeat with **cat**.

★ **Spelling Pictures** Children picture-code and illustrate **cat** and **hat**.

★ **Assessment** Plan an assessment <u>one week from now</u>. Use *Activity Sheet 1: Sort words according to initial sound*, and/or *Activity Sheet 6: Write letter in response to picture*. (See page 26.)

**Spelling Picture**

N.B. **Spelling Pictures**
Keep these sheets for a take-home book of words that children can show to their families once completed. (Page 31.)

## (6) Topics

See p29

★ **Numbers** Teach the number **ten** and the word **fingers**, using your ten fingers. Use number cards **1-10** in a game of 'What's missing?' (page 85).

★ **Student Book & CD** Pages 24 and 25 (How many fingers?)

## (7) Review & pair work

★ **Workbook** Pages 12 and 13. Children could attempt the counting exercises on page 13 in pairs.

# Sammy Snake

## TEACHING OBJECTIVES:

✔ **s** and **S** letter shapes and sound
✔ Sammy Snake's words: snake, sun, seven
✔ Extension words: sandwiches, sandcastle, seal
✔ Oral vocabulary: How are you? I'm happy. I'm sad.
✔ Word building: sad, hats, cats
✔ Spelling picture: cats

## YOU'LL NEED:

✔ Prepare a tune for 'Sammy's Seaside Song' ③
✔ Paper for 'Spelling pictures' ⑤
✔ Pictures of happy and sad people ⑥

## 1 Keyword: snake

See p16

★ **What's in the box?** Look in the box and mime the movement of a snak[e] with your hand as you hiss: 'Sss…'. It's a sssnake. Then take the toy o[r] card out of the box. (Tip: Really emphasise Sammy Snake's 'sss…' soun[d] at the beginning of words in this lesson.)

## 2 Letter sound

See p17-1[]

Action

★ **Sammy Snake** Can you find a snake on the wall frieze? Good! This is Sammy Snake. Sammy Snake lives in Letterland.

★ **Theme Song** Go to Letterland!

★ **Sound** Use the *Big Picture Code Crad* and the Sounds Trick to discover SammySnake's letter sound: Sammy Snake, 'sss…'*

★ **Action** Teach Sammy Snake's Action Trick.

★ **Alphabet Song** Sing SS's *Alphabet Song*. Show the picture-side of his *Car[d]* when you sing his name and the plain letter side when you 'hiss' his sound[.]

★ **Picture-code** Children add Sammy Snake's picture details to a plain black **s**

## 3 Sammy Snake's words

See p20-2[]

**\*Sleeping Sammy**:
Sammy is needed in so many words that he sometimes has a quick snooze to catch up on lost sleep. Then you'll hear his sleeping 'zzz…' sound. For example, in words like **is**, **his**, **was**, **boys**, **girls**, etc.

★ **Present** Use *Vocabulary Cards* to introduce the words: **snake**, **sun** and **seven**

★ **Use new words** Use new words in a game of 'Listen & jump' (page 84).

★ *Extension: **'Sammy's Seaside Song'***. Make up your own tune, or chant the words together. Add an action for each verb.

*I like to…   swim in the sea, sit in the sun,*
*              eat sandwiches, yum, yum, yum,*
*              swim in the sea, sit in the sun,*
*              eat sandwiches, yum, yum, yum!*

★ **Student Book & CD** Pages 26 and 27

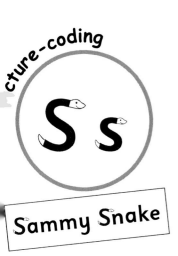

**cture-coding**

**Sammy Snake**

## 4  Letter shapes

See p22-24

★ **Find the letter** Write some letters on the board, including a few previously taught letters and an **s**. *Can you find Sammy Snake's letter?* etc…

★ **Form the letter** Write a big **s** on the board, picture-code it and air-trace it together. *Start at Sammy Snake's head.* Repeat with a plain letter. *Where is Sammy Snake's head?* Make sure Sammy Snake can slither off in the Reading Direction! (*Optional:* Use Sammy's handwriting verse.)

★ **Capital letter** Write and picture-code lower case and capital **s** & **S** on the board. Demonstrate or translate the capital letter story: **When Sammy has a chance to start an important word, like a name, he takes a deep breath and gets bigger – like a Super Snake!** Notice that his capital letter appears TWICE in his own name.

★ **Handwriting Book** Pages 14 and 15

**Live Reading**

## 5  Phonemic awareness & phonics

See p25-28

★ **Word sort & letter line** Try the role-play activity on page 25. Or choose another Revision game (e.g. 'Who am I… ?').

★ **Workbook** Page 14 (or save it for a review activity at the end of the lesson).

★ **Live Reading** Hand out Sammy Snake, Annie Apple and Dippy Duck *Big Picture Code Cards.* Line up the children under the Reading Direction sign, to create the word **sad**. Then help them to blend the sounds and read the word.

**Spelling Picture**

★ *Extension:* **Live Spelling** Take in the cards and hand out CC, AA, TT, HHM and SS *Card's.* 'Slow-speak' the word **hat** (hhha…t) and ask the children to decide who needs to be in the word, in which order. Then slow-speak the word **hats** and ask which new letter child is needed to complete the word. Repeat with **cat** / **cats**.

★ **Spelling Picture** Children picture-code and illustrate the words **cats**.

**Happy/sad**

## 6  Topics

See p29

★ **Happy / sad** Teach the following sentences to prepare for the *Student Book* activities: **How are you? I am / He is / She is (happy / sad).** Use your own facial expressions and /or pictures of happy and sad people. Follow up with a game of 'Mood words' (page 84).

★ **Student Book & CD** Pages 28 and 29

## 7  Review & pair work

See p29

★ **Workbook** Pages 14 and 15. Children could attempt both pages in pairs.

# Impy Ink & Mr I

## TEACHING OBJECTIVES:

✔ **i** and **I** letter shapes and sounds (long and short)
✔ Impy Ink's words: insect, ink, in
✔ Extension words: interesting, imagination, ice-cream
✔ Oral vocabulary: in / on ; How many legs?

## YOU'LL NEED:

✔ Ice-cream: use a paper cone & tissue paper ice-cream ③
✔ All *Name Flashcards* ⑤
✔ Toy or paper insect ⑥

## 1 Keyword: ink

See p16

★ **What's in the box?** Try to get a bottle of **ink**. If possible, use an ink pen to demonstrate what we do with ink. **It's ink.** To check understanding, show crayons, pens and pencils and ask: **Is this ink?** You may even be able to get hold of invisible ink!

## 2 Letter sound

See p17-

★ **Impy Ink** Can you find any ink on the wall frieze? Good! This is Impy Ink. Impy Ink lives in Letterland. (All the children in Letterland write with ink that Impy Ink gives them.)

★ **Theme Song** Go to Letterland!

★ **Sound** Discover his letter sound: Impy Ink, 'ĭ...'

★ **Action** Teach Impy Ink's Action Trick.

★ **Alphabet Song** (See previous lesson.)

★ **Picture-code** Children add Impy Ink's picture details to a plain black **i**.

## 3 Impy Ink's words & Mr I

See p20-2

★ **Present** Use *Vocabulary Cards* to introduce the words: **ink**, **insect** and **in**.

★ **Use new words** Use the new words in a game of 'What's missing?' (page 85)

★ **Student Book & CD** Pages 30 and 31. Use the *Big Picture Code Cards* and the scene on page 31 of the SB to introduce Mr I, the Ice-cream Man. Mr I is holding an ice-cream at the bottom of page 31 of the SB, because he sells ice-cream to all the children in Letterland. Teach the word **ice-cream** using your paper ice-cream prop. You could also make Mr I's gesture: punch the air with the ice-cream prop and say his name, 'I!' (pronounced 'eye'). Review Mr A and his action as well (page 83).

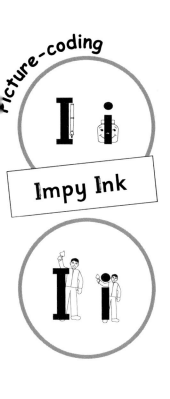

Picture-coding

**I i**

Impy Ink

**I i**

## ④ Letter shapes

See p22-24

★ **Find the letter**  Write some letters on the board, including a few previously taught letters and an **i**. Can you find Impy Ink's letter? etc...

★ **Form the letter**  Write a big **i** on the board, picture-code it and air-trace it together. Start at the top. Go down. Then add his dot. Repeat with a plain letter. (*Optional*: Use Impy Ink's handwriting verse.)

★ **Capital letter**  Write and picture-code lower case and capital **i** & **I** on the board. Demonstrate or translate the capital letter story: When Impy Ink has a chance to start important words, he uses his tall thin ink pen to do the job for him. Notice that his capital letter appears TWICE in his own name. When Mr I starts an important word, he just stands next to his capital letter and says his name, 'I!' (eye).

★ **Handwriting Book**  Pages 16 and 17

## ⑤ Phonemic awareness

See p25-28

★ **Word sort & letter line**  Try the cumulative role-play activity on page 25. *Variation*: Use Name Flashcards intead of *Vocabulary Cards* (E.g. I'm Clever Cat. This is my name.)  To help children read the character names, remind them of the character names trick (page 17).

★ **Workbook**  Page 16 (or save it for a review activity at the end of the lesson.)

In & on

## ⑥ Topics

See p29

★ **In & on**  Teach the following vocabulary in preparation for page 32 of the *Student Book*: The insect is in / on the box. Use a box and a toy or paper insect tied to a string. Chant the 'In & On Song':

> Now the insect's IN *the box*, IN *the box*, IN *the box*.
> Now the insect's IN *the box*, IN THE BOX!
> Now the insect's ON *the box*, ON *the box*, ON *the box*.
> Now the insect's ON *the box*, ON THE BOX!
> IN *the box*, ON *the box*, IN *the box*, ON *the box*...
> Now the insect's IN *the box*, IN THE BOX!

★ **How many legs?**  Teach the word **legs** and count six legs on a chalkboard drawing of an insect.

★ **Student Book & CD**  Pages 32 and 33

## ⑦ Review & pair work

See p29

★ **Workbook**  Pages 16 and 17. Children could attempt both pages in pairs.

# Noisy Nick

## TEACHING OBJECTIVES:

✔ **n** and **N** letter shapes and sound
✔ Noisy Nick's words: nest, nine, nut
✔ Extension words: numbers, net, nails, noisy
✔ Oral vocabulary: How old are you? I am…years old.

## YOU'LL NEED:

✔ Nine nuts ①
✔ Also: See checklist on page 35

### 1 Keyword: nine

Se
p1c

★ **What's in the box?** Put the number **9** Vocabulary Card in the box. **It's th₀
number nine.** Ask some children: **How old are you? (I am …years old.**
You could also put nine nuts in the box and count them too. Turn th₀
Vocabulary Card over so children can see Noisy Nick starting the word **nin₀**

### 2 Letter sound

See
p17-

★ **Noisy Nick** Show Noisy Nick on the back of the 9 Vocabulary Card. **Can you
find this boy on the wall frieze? Good! This is Noisy Nick. Noisy Nick
lives in Letterland. He is nine years old.** (He's called Noisy Nick because
he has a lot of noisy habits, like banging nails and banging drums.)

★ **Sound** Use the Big Picture Code Cards and the Sounds Trick to discover NN's
letter sound: **Noisy Nick, 'nnn…'**

★ **Action** Teach Noisy Nick's Actions Trick.

★ **Review** Do a 'Quick Dash' (page 19) through all the letter sounds anₐ
actions you have taught so far.

★ **Alphabet Song** Sing NN's ELT Alphabet Song. Show the picture-side of hiₛ
Big Picture Code Cards when you sing his name and the plain letter side when yoᵤ
make his sound.

Action

### 3 Noisy Nick's words

See
p20-

★ **Picture-code** Children add Noisy Nick's picture details to a plain black **n**

★ **Present** Use Vocabulary Cards to introduce: **nest**, **nine** and **nut**.

★ **Use new words** Use the new words in a game of 'Shuffle cards' (page 85).

★ **Student Book & CD** Pages 34 and 35. Make sure you point out the nailₛ
in the scene on page 35. The word **nails** will help you explain the correcₜ
way to form Noisy Nick's lower case and capital letter. (See top of next page.

Picture-coding

**N n**

Noisy Nick

Letter Line

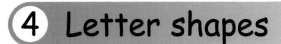

## ④ Letter shapes

See p22-24

★ **Find the letter** Write some letters on the board, including a few previously taught letters and an **n**. Can you find Noisy Nick's letter? etc…

★ **Form the letter** Write a big **n** on the board, picture-code it and air-trace it together. To give children the correct starting position say: Draw Noisy Nick's nail. (*Optional*: Use Noisy Nick's handwriting verse.)

★ **Capital letter** Write and picture-code lower case and capital **n** & **N** on the board. Demonstrate or translate the capital letter story: **To make his capital letter, Noisy Nick bangs three long and straight nails together, like this…** Notice that his capital letter appears TWICE in his own name.

★ **Handwriting Book** Pages 18 and 19

## ⑤ Phonemic awareness

See p25-28

★ **Word sort & letter line** Try the cumulative role-play activity on page 25.

★ **Workbook** Page 18 (or save it for a review activity at the end of the lesson.)

## ⑥ Topics

See p29

★ **Numbers** Play 'Noisy Nines': Go around the class saying the numbers **1** to **10**. Each child whispers their number, except for the child who shouts 'NINE!' Go back to **1** after the number **10**, and continue playing.

★ **Student Book & CD** Pages 36 and 37

## ⑦ Review & pair work

See p29

★ **Workbook** Pages 18 and 19. Children could attempt both pages in pairs.

Noisy Nines

NINE!

# Oscar Orange & Mr O

## TEACHING OBJECTIVES:

✔ **o** and **O** letter shapes and sounds (long and short)
✔ Oscar Orange's words: orange, octopus, ostrich
✔ Extension words: on, office, old
✔ Oral vocabulary: triangle, circle, square; red, orange, yellow, green; Please give me a...

## YOU'LL NEED:

✔ A fresh orange ①
✔ OO & AA cards ⑤
✔ Make up a tune for the 'Orange & Apple Song' ⑥
✔ Red, orange & yellow cut-outs of triangles, circles & squares ⑥

### ① Keyword: orange

See p16

★ **What's in the box?** Put an orange in the box. **It's an orange.** Review **o** and **in** by placing the orange in and on the box. (See Section 6 for a chant.) Explain that 'orange' is also the name for a colour. Review the colours **red**, **orange**, **yellow** and **green** by pointing at objects in the classroom and asking: **Is this red / orange / yellow / green?**

### ② Letter sound

See p17-1

★ **Oscar Orange** Can you find an orange on the wall frieze? Good! This is Oscar Orange. Oscar Orange lives in Letterland. (If possible, explain that he is a talking orange – not an eating orange.)

★ **Sound** Sounds Trick: Oscar Orange, 'o...'

★ **Action** Teach Oscar Orange's Action Trick.

★ **Review** Do a 'Quick Dash' (page 19) through all the letter sounds and actions you have learnt so far.

★ **Alphabet Song** (See previous lesson.)

★ **Picture-code** Children add Oscar Orange's picture details to a plain black **o**, and colour him orange.

*Action*
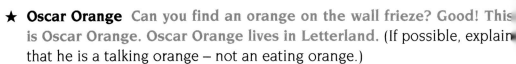

### ③ Oscar Orange's words & Mr O

See p20-2

★ **Present** Use *Vocabulary Cards* to introduce the words: **orange, octopus & ostrich**

★ **Use new words** Use the new words in a game of 'Shuffle cards' (page 85).

★ **Student Book & CD** Pages 38 and 39. Use the *Big Picture Code Cards* and the scene on SB page 39 to introduce Mr O, the Old Man who works at the Letterland docks. Mr O's letters are the same shape as Oscar's letters, but he says his name, 'oh!' in words instead. Teach the word **old** as an example of a word that begins his sound. Teach his Action Trick (page 83)

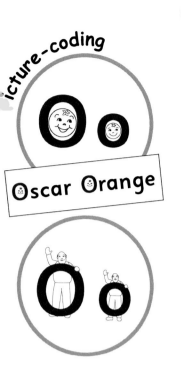

picture-coding

Oscar Orange

## ④ Letter shape

See p22-24

★ **Find the letter** Write some letters on the board, including a few previously taught letters and an **o**. Can you find Oscar Orange's letter? etc…

★ **Form the letter** Write a big **o** on the board, picture-code it and air-trace it together. Start over his eye. It's the same place that Annie Apple's letter starts - by the leaf. (Optional: Use Oscar Orange's handwriting verse.)

★ **Capital letter** Write and picture-code a lower case and capital **o** & **O** on the board. Demonstrate or translate the capital letter story: When Oscar Orange has a chance to start an important word, he takes a deep breath and gets bigger. Notice that Oscar Orange's capital letter appears TWICE in his own name. When Mr O starts an important word, he stands next to his capital letter and says his name, 'oh!'

★ **Handwriting Book** Pages 20 and 21

## ⑤ Phonemic awareness & phonics

See p25-28

★ **Word sort & letter line** Try the cumulative role-play activity on page 25. Alternatively, choose another Revision game from the Activity Bank.

★ **Workbook** Page 20 (or save it for a review activity at the end of the lesson.)

★ **Short vowels** Give each child an Annie Apple and an Oscar Orange card (pages 91-92). Say each word below and ask children whether they hear Oscar Orange or Annie Apple's sound *inside* the word. They hold up the correct card. **hot, hat / pot, pat / mop, map / top, tap**

★ **Live Reading & Spelling** Help children to build these words:
**on–> in–> it–> sit –> hit**

## ⑥ Topics

See pp 32

colours & shapes

red

orange    yellow

★ **Colours & verbs** Make up a tune for the **'Orange and Apple Song'**, or chant:
> My orange is orange, my apple is red.
> Turn around and touch your head.
> My orange is orange, my apple is red.
> Clap, clap, clap and touch your head.
> My orange is orange, my apple is red.
> Hop, hop, hop and touch your head.

★ **Shapes** Introduce the words **triangle**, **circle** and **square** using cut-outs. Play 'Guess the Shape': Put 3 squares (red, orange, yellow), 3 circles and 3 triangles in a bag. Pupils take turns to put their hands in the bag, choose a cut-out, feel it and guess the shape, e.g: It's a square. Then they guess the colour and say both shape and colour aloud before pulling it out, e.g: It's a red square. The class confirms or corrects the guess.

★ **Student Book & CD** Pages 40 and 41

## ⑦ Review & pair work

See pp 32

★ **Workbook** Pages 20 and 21. Children could attempt both pages in pairs.

# Peter Puppy

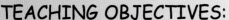

## Lesson 11

**TEACHING OBJECTIVES:**

✔ **p** and **P** letter shapes and sound
✔ Peter Puppy's words: paint, parrot, pig
✔ Extension words: paintbrush, picture, people, penguin
✔ Oral vocabulary: person, people; pink, purple; I can…
paint, jump, drink, eat, sleep, swim, read; his/her name…

**YOU'LL NEED:**

✔ Jar of pink paint, jar of purple paint and paintbrush ①
✔ Pictures of individuals and groups of people ⑥
✔ Also: See the checklist on page 35

## ① Keywords: pink / purple paint

See p1(

★ **What's in the box?** Put a jar of pink paint and a jar of purple paint in the box. **It's paint. This is pink paint. This is purple paint.** Paint Peter Puppy's pink letter on a piece of paper.

## ② Letter sound

See p20-2

★ **Peter Puppy** **Can you find a pink letter on the wall frieze? Good! This is Peter Puppy. Peter Puppy lives in Letterland.** (If possible, explain that a puppy is a young dog. Admire Peter Puppy's long droopy ears. He always hopes that his ears will prick up, but they are always droopy. His droopy ears will help you to explain later on, why his lower case letter always drops below the line!)

★ **Theme Song** Go to Letterland!

★ **Sound** Use the *Big Picture Code Card* and the Sounds Trick to discover Peter Puppy's letter sound: **Peter Puppy, 'p…'**

★ **Action** Teach Peter Puppy's Action Trick.

★ **Alphabet Song** Sing PP's ELT *Alphabet Song.* Show the picture-side of his *Car* when you sing his name and the plain letter side when you whisper his sound

★ **Picture-code** Children add Peter Puppy's picture details to a plain black **p**.

★ **Assessment** You have now introduced the next set of 5 letter sounds. You may like to plan to assess these 5 letter sounds <u>one week from now</u>. Sa the letter sound in response to the plain letters: s,i,n,o,p. (See page 19.)

## ③ Peter Puppy's words

See p20-2

★ **Present** Use *Vocabulary Cards* to introduce: **paint, parrot** and **pig**.

★ **Use new words** Choose an activity from the Activity Bank to give children ar opportunity to use the new words. Suggestion: 'What's missing?' (page 85).

★ **Student Book & CD** Pages 42 and 43

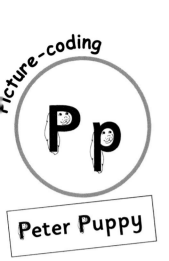

Picture-coding

P p

Peter Puppy

## 4 Letter shapes

See p22-24

★ **Find the letter** Write some letters on the board, including a few previously taught letters and a **p**. **Can you find Peter Puppy's letter?** etc…

★ **Form the letter** Write a big **p** on the board, picture-code it and air-trace it together. **First draw PP's droopy ears…**

★ **Capital letter** Write and picture-code a lower case and capital **p** & **P** on the board. Demonstrate or translate the capital letter story: **When Peter Puppy has a chance to start an important word, he is so pleased that he pops up so that everyone can see him better, and then his whole letter is above the line.** Notice that his capital letter appears TWICE in his own name.

★ **Handwriting Book** Pages 22 and 23

★ **Assessment** You have now taught the next 5 letter shapes. Plan to assess them <u>one week from now</u>. *Write letter in response to a sound:* s,i,o,n,p. (See page 24.)

## 5 Phonemic awareness

See p25-28

★ **Word sort & letter line** Try the cumulative role-play activity on page 28. Alternatively, choose another Revision game from the Activity Bank.

★ **Workbook** Page 22 (or save it for a review activity at the end of the lesson).

★ **Assessment** Plan an assessment <u>one week from now</u>. Use *Activity Sheet 2: Sort words according to initial sound,* and/or *Activity Sheet 7: Write letter in response to picture.* (See page 26.)

## 6 Topics

See p29

Verbs

★ **Person / people** Teach the words **person** and **people** in preparation for the *Student Book* activities. Show a series of pictures of individuals and people. Children call out: **person** or **people**.

★ **I can…(verb)** To prepare for SB page 45, teach gestures & words for the following verbs - (children know some of them from previous lessons): **paint, read, drink, eat** (lick an ice-cream), **swim, sleep** & **jump.** Call out one sentence at a time and ask children to repeat the sentence and make the gesture: **I can jump. I can read.** etc…

★ **Student Book & CD** Pages 44 and 45

★ **Her / His name is…** Show each *Big Picture Code Card* and give each child a chance to use the phrase: **His / Her name is…** (Clever Cat, Annie Apple, Harry Hat Man) etc… in preparation for the *Workbook* activity on page 23.

## 7 Review & pair work

See p32

★ **Workbook** Pages 22 and 23. Children could attempt both pages in pairs.

# Yellow Yo-yo Man & Golden Girl

### Lesson 12

## TEACHING OBJECTIVES:

✔ **yY** and **gG** letter shapes and sounds
✔ Yo-yo Man's words: yellow, yo-yo, yoghurt
✔ Golden Girl's words: girl, green, grapes, goat
✔ Oral vocabulary: big, little; up, down, around; boy, man, girl, woman, grow; is wearing

## YOU'LL NEED:

✔ Pictures of girls, boys, men, women ①
✔ Pictures of things that grow and things that don't grow ⑥
✔ Also: See the checklist on page 35

## ① Keywords: girl, yellow

See p16

★ **Keywords** First teach the words **girl**, and review **yellow**. Use pictures or draw stick figures on the board to represent **girl**. You could also introduce the words **boy**, **man**, **woman**, **big** and **little** at this stage. Check understanding using pictures: **Is this a girl? Is this a man?**

## ② Letter sounds

See p17-

★ **YYM & GG** Can you find a man with a yellow letter on the wall frieze? Yyyes! Can you find a girl with a green letter? Good! This is Yellow Yo-yo Man and this is Golden Girl. They live in Letterland.

★ **Sounds** Sounds Tricks: Yellow Yo-yo Man, 'yyy…'; Golden Girl, 'g…'

★ **Review** Do a 'Quick Dash' (page 19) through all the letter sounds and actions you have taught so far.

★ **Actions** Teach both Action Tricks (pages 82-83).

★ **Alphabet Songs** Sing the ELT *Alphabet Songs*, one at a time. Show the picture-side of the *Big Picture Code Card* when you sing the character name and the plain letter side when you make the letter sound.

★ **Picture-code** Children add each Letterlander's picture details to plain black letters.

N.B. **Letter shapes**
Teach whichever shape you prefer: 'y' or 'y'.

## ③ YYM & GG's words

See p20-

★ **Present** Use *Vocabulary Cards* to introduce: **yo-yo**, **yellow**, **yoghurt**; **green**, **grapes** and **goat**. In each case ask children to decide whether the word starts with YYM's sound or GG's sound before you put the word in a sentence. Yo-yo Man likes to eat yoghurt. Golden Girl likes to eat grapes. etc…

★ **Use new words** Use the new words in a game of 'Order Please!' (page 84)

★ **Student Book & CD** Pages 46 and 47.

Picture-coding

**Yo-yo Man**

Picture-coding

**Golden Girl**

See
p22-24

## (4) Letter shapes

★ **Find the letters** Can you find Yellow Yo-yo Man's letter? Where is Golden Girl's letter? etc…(As in previous lessons.)

★ **Form the letters** (As in previous lessons.) Start by making YYM's sack. Start at GG's head… The starting point for the **g** is the same as AA's letter. (*Optional*: Use handwriting verses.)

★ **Capital letters** Write and picture-code lower case and capital **y** & **Y** and **g** & **G** on the board. Demonstrate or translate the capital letter stories: **GG always gets into her go-kart to start a name. In her swing she is not looking in the Reading Direction (it makes her giddy), but in her go-kart, she has to see where she is going, so she does face the Reading Direction! When YYM starts an important word, he quickly empties out his heavy yo-yo's so that he can step up onto the line to show us how important his word is.** Notice that the characters' capital letters appear TWICE in their own names.

★ **Handwriting Book** Pages 24, 25, 26 and 27

See
p25-28

## (5) Phonemic awareness

★ **Word sort & letter line** Try the cumulative role-play activity on page 25.

★ **Workbook** Page 24 (or save it for a review activity at the end of the lesson).

See
p29

## (6) Topics

up, down & around

★ **Big / little / grow** Teach the words **big**, **little** and **grow**. Use chalkboard drawings or cut-outs, and/or mime a growing flower. I'm a little flower. I'm growing. Now I'm a big flower. Show a series of pictures or *Vocabulary Cards*. Can an apple grow? Can an acrobat grow? Can a car grow? Can a hat grow? Children could pretend to grow from little to big. A little apple can grow and grow … into a big apple. etc…

★ **Student Book & CD** page 48

★ **up / down / around** Teach **up**, **down** and **around**, then play a game of 'Golden Girl says… stand up / sit down, turn around'. Alternatively, play 'Up, down and around': Noses UP! …and down…up, down, up, down. Arms UP!…and down…up, down, up, down. Noses UP!…and around, around, around. etc…

★ **Student Book and CD** page 49

See
p29

## (7) Review & pair work

★ **Workbook** Pages 24 and 25. Children could attempt both pages in pairs.

# Eddy Elephant & Mr E
# Uppy Umbrella & Mr U

### Lesson 13

**TEACHING OBJECTIVES:**

✔ **eE** and **uU** letter shapes and sounds
✔ Eddy Elephant's words: elephant, egg, elbow
✔ Uppy Umbrella's words: umbrella, up, under
✔ Oral vocabulary: in, on and under
✔ Word-building: ten, net, nest, net, nut, sun, up; hat, hit, hot, hut; pan, pen, pin and more...
✔ Spelling pictures: ten, up

**YOU'LL NEED:**

✔ Umbrella ①
✔ Sentence-building copymaster ⑥
✔ Also: See the checklist on page 35

## ① Keywords: umbrella, elephant
<small>See p16</small>

★ **What's in the box?** What's in the box? There's nothing IN the box, but what is UNDER the box? It's an umbrella! Check understanding by pointing at objects and asking: Is this an umbrella? Show the elephant *Vocabulary Card*: Is this an umbrella? No! This is an elephant. Children repeat the word **elephant**

## ② Letter sounds
<small>See p17-</small>

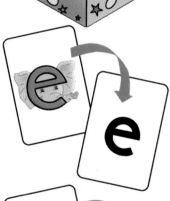

★ **EE & UU** Can you find an elephant on the wall frieze? Good! This is Eddy Elephant. He lives in Letterland. Can you find an umbrella? This is Uppy Umbrella. She lives in Letterland.

★ **Sounds** Eddy Elephant, 'ĕ...'; Uppy Umbrella, 'ŭ...'

★ **Actions** Teach both Action Tricks (pages 82-83).

★ **Alphabet Songs** (See previous lesson.)

★ **Picture-code** Children add Letterlander's picture details to plain black letters

## ③ EE & UU's words, Mr E & Mr U
<small>See p20-2</small>

★ **Present** Use *Vocabulary Cards* to introduce the words: **elephant**, **egg**, **elbow**, **umbrella**, **up** and **under**. Ask children to decide whether each word starts with Eddy's or Uppy's sound before you put it in a sentence, e.g. **Eddy Elephant likes to eat eggs. Uppy Umbrella likes to go up in the sky.**

★ **Use new words** Use the new words in a game of 'What's missing?' (page 85)

★ **Vowel Men** Use *Cards* to introduce Mr E the Easy Magic Man (he owns EE) and Mr U the Uniform Man (he owns UU). Review the Vowel Men's Action Trick (page 83). Then review *all* the long and short vowels.

★ **Student Book & CD** Pages 50, 51 and 52

picture-coding

Eddy Elephant

picture-coding

Uppy Umbrella

Vowels-go-round

See p22-24

## 4 Letter shapes

★ **Find the letters & form the letters** (See previous lesson.)

★ **Capital letters** Write and picture-code lower case and uppercase **e** & **E** and **u** & **U** on the board. Demonstrate or translate the capital letter stories: When Eddy Elephant starts an important word, he sits down and points everything – his trunk and all his feet – in the Reading Direction! Like everyone else in Letterland, Uppy Umbrella loves to start important words. All she has to do to get bigger is to take a deep breath. Notice that the characters' capital letters appear TWICE in their own names.

★ **Vowel Men** When the Vowel Men start important words, they stand next to their capital letters and say their names, 'ee!' or 'you!'

★ **Handwriting Book** Pages 28, 29, 30 and 31

See p25-28

## 5 Phonemic awareness & phonics

★ **Word sort & letter line** Try the cumulative role-play activity on page 25.

★ **Workbook** Page 26 (or save it for a review activity at the end of the lesson).

★ **Live Reading & Live Spelling** First review all the short vowel sounds with a 'Quick Dash' (page 19). Then do some Live Reading using 'Vowels-go-round' (page 87). Finally, do some Live Spelling using the following word chain: **ten–> net–> nest–> net–> nut–> nuts–> sun–> up**

★ **Spelling pictures** Children picture-code and illustrate the words **ten** and **up**.

★ **Student Book & CD** Page 53

Sentence-building

See p29

## 6 Topics & sentence-building

★ **On / in / under** Give each child a photocopy of the words and pictures on the sentence-building copymaster (page 106). (Use enlarged copies for a demonstration.) Demonstrate one sentence on the board by saying a sentence out loud and putting up the cards in the correct order. Then read out the remaining sentences one at a time: The elephant is on the box. The elephant is under the box. The umbrella is under the box. The umbrella is in the box. Children choose the appropriate pictures and words and put them in the correct order on their desks.

★ **Up / down / around** Play 'Up, down and around' (page 59) again, this time include elbows.

## 7 Review & pair work

★ **Workbook** Pages 26 and 27. Children could attempt both pages in pairs.

# Kicking King & Quarrelsome Queen
## Lesson 14

### TEACHING OBJECTIVES:

✔ **Kk** and **Qq** letter shapes and sounds
✔ Keywords: king, queen
✔ KK & QQ's words: key, kangaroo, kite; quill, question, quilt
✔ Listening vocabulary: Who is / has / likes / can…?
✔ Word-building: kick, sick, stick, sock, dock, duck, ducks, quick
✔ Spelling picture: ducks

### YOU'LL NEED:

✔ King and queen keyword props, e.g. crowns, robes, storybook or pictures ①
✔ Also: See the checklist on page 35

## 1 Keywords: king, queen

See p16

★ **What's in the box?** Ideas for keyword objects: Props that a king and queen would use, e.g. crowns and robes; a storybook about a king and queen o pictures of kings and queens from a variety of cultures.

## 2 Letter sounds

See p17-1

★ **KK and QQ** Can you find a king on the wall frieze? Can you find a queen? Good! This is Kicking King and this is Quarrelsome Queen. They live in the Letterland castle. QQ does not face the Reading Direction like all the other Letterlanders. She is too quarrelsome!

★ **Sounds** Kicking King, 'k…'*; Quarrelsome Queen, 'qu…' Draw attention to the differences in mouth shapes to help contrast the 'k…' and 'qu…' sounds.

★ **Action** Teach both Action Tricks (pages 82-83).

★ **Alphabet Songs** As in previous lessons. Sing the songs and show the Cards

★ **Picture-code** Children add picture details to plain letters.

★ **Assessment** You have now introduced 6 more sounds. You may like to plan to assess these 5 letter sounds <u>one week from now</u>. *Say the letter sound in response to the plain letters*: y,g,e,u,k,q. (See page 19.)

## 3 KK & QQ's words

See p20-2

*\*N.B. KK makes exactly the same sound as CC. But KK usually appears at the end of words – CC starts far more words than KK.*

★ **Present** Use *Vocabulary Cards* to introduce: **key**, **kangaroo**, **kite**, **quill question** and **quilt**. Ask children whether each word starts with KK's sound or QQ's sound before you put the word in a sentence, e.g. Kicking King likes kangaroos. Quarrelsome Queen likes to ask questions. etc…

★ **Use new words** Choose an activity from the Activity Bank. Suggestion 'What's missing?' (page 85).

★ **Student Book & CD** Pages 54 and 55.

Picture-coding

**K k**

Kicking King

Picture-coding

**Q q**

Quarrelsome Queen

Spelling Picture

ducks

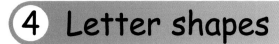

## ④ Letter shapes

See p22-24

★ **Find the letters & form the letters** (See Lesson 13.)

★ **Capital letters** Write and picture-code lower case and uppercase **k** & **K** and **q** & **Q** on the board. Demonstrate or translate the capital letter stories: **When Kicking King starts an important word, he takes a deep breath and gets bigger! When Quarrelsome Queen starts an important word, she goes into her Quiet Room and sits very quietly as she says, 'qu…'.** Notice that the characters' capital letters appear TWICE in their own names.

★ **Handwriting Book** Pages 32, 33, 34 and 35

★ **Assessment** You have now taught 6 more letter shapes. You have now taught the next 5 letter shapes. Plan to assess them <u>one week from now</u>. *Write letter in response to a sound*: y,g,e,u,k,q. (See page 24.)

## ⑤ Phonemic awareness & phonics

See p25-28

★ **Word sort & letter line** Try the cumulative role-play activity on page 25. Alternatively, play 'Knock, knock' (page 86).

★ **Workbook** Page 28 (or save it for a review activity at the end of the lesson).

★ **Live Reading & Live Spelling** Write these letters on the board: **c**, **k**, **-ck**. Explain that they all make the same sound. (CC loves to stand behind KK, where it is safe, and watch him practise his kicks in short, quick words like **kick**, **duck** and **sock**. Use the following word chain for Live Reading and/or Spelling: **kick–> sick–> stick–> sick–> sock–> dock–> duck–> ducks–> quick**

★ **Spelling picture** Children picture-code and illustrate the word **ducks**.

★ **Student Book & CD** Page 57

★ **Assessment** Plan an assessment <u>one week from now</u>. Use *Activity Sheet 3: Sort words according to initial sound*, and/or *Activity Sheet 8: Write letter in response to picture*. (See page 26.)

## ⑥ Topics

See p29

★ **Questions** Give each pair of children one or two *Big Picture Code Cards*. Children with the relevant *Cards* (may be more than one) stand up & answer the question:

Who has a red letter?              Who likes to swim in the sea?
Who likes to eat magnets?      Who has three legs?
Who likes to talk on her telephone?   Who is nine years old?  etc…

★ **Student Book & CD** Page 56

## ⑦ Review & pair work

See p29

★ **Workbook** Pages 28 and 29. Children could attempt both pages in pairs.

# Firefighter Fred & Red Robot

### Lesson 15

## TEACHING OBJECTIVES:

✔ **fF** and **rR** letter shapes and sounds
✔ Firefighter Fred's words: fire, flowers, fish
✔ Red Robot's words: red, rocket, ring
✔ Oral vocabulary: My favourite food is… Who am I?
✔ Word-building: fun, sun, run, red, Fred
✔ Spelling picture: sun

## YOU'LL NEED:

✔ Red ring, ring box + note ①
✔ Rice and fruit ⑤
✔ Also: See the checklist on page 35

## ① Keywords: fire, red ring

See p16

★ **What's in the box?** Put the **fire** *Vocabulary* Card in the box and a small, empty ring box. Stick a toy ring (red if possible) above Red Robot on the wall frieze for children to find later. To introduce **fire**, pretend the box is hot. **It's hot!** Take out the **fire** card. **It's fire! Where is Firefighter Fred?** After you have met FF, look in the box again. Take out the ring box and 'read' this note in a robot voice: **Hello** (your name). **I am red. I am a robot. I have your red ring!**

## ② Letter sounds

See p17-1

★ **FF & RR** This is Firefighter Fred. He puts out fires. Firefighter Fred lives in Letterland. Look! This is my ring! Red Robot has my red ring! (He likes to run off with things that begin with rrr…'!)

★ **Sounds** Firefighter Fred 'fff…'; Red Robot, 'rrr…'

★ **Actions** Teach both Action Tricks (pages 82-83).

★ **Review** Do a 'Quick Dash' (page 19) through all the letter sounds and actions you have learnt so far.

★ **Alphabet Songs** Sing the ELT *Alphabet Songs* and show the *Cards*.

★ **Picture-code** Children add each Letterlander's picture details to a plain black letter.

## ③ FF & RR's words

See p20-2

★ **Present** Use *Vocabulary Cards* to introduce: **fire, flowers, fish, red, rocket** and **ring**. Ask children whether each word starts with FF's 'fff…' sound or RR's 'rrr…' sound before you put it in a sentence, e.g. **Firefighter Fred has five pet fish. Red Robot likes the colour red.** etc…

★ **Use new words** Use the words in a game of 'Draw and say' (page 84).

★ **Student Book & CD** Pages 58 and 59.

Picture-coding

Firefighter Fred

Red Robot

Live Spelling

Spelling Picture

Favourite foods

**(4) Letter shapes**

See p22-24

★ **Find the letters & form the letters** (See Lesson 13.)

★ **Capital letters** Write and picture-code lower case and uppercase **f** & **F** and **r** & **R** on the board. Demonstrate or translate the capital letter stories: *Firefighter Fred makes his letter straighter and sharper to start an important word. Red Robot takes a deep breath and gets bigger AND he changes his shape, so it is even more difficult to catch him. But we won't be fooled!* Notice that the characters' capital letters appear TWICE in their own names.

★ **Handwriting Book** Pages 36, 37, 38 and 39

**(5) Phonemic awareness & phonics**

See p25-28

★ **Word sort & letter line** Try the cumulative role-play activity on page 25.

★ **Workbook** Page 30 (or save it for a review activity at the end of the lesson). (You'll need to pre-teach the words **rice** and **fruit** for this activity.)

★ **Live Spelling** Hand out *Big Picture Code Cards* **f**, **n**, **r**, **s**, **e**, **d** and **u**. 'Slow-speak' the word **sun** (sssunnn) and help children to build the word at the front of the class. Next slow-speak the word **fun** and ask who needs to sit down and who needs to come up to make the new word. Repeat with **run**. Show children how to build the name **Fred** by adding a capital **F** to the word **red**.

★ **Spelling Picture** Children picture-code and illustrate the word **sun**.

★ **Student Book & CD** Page 61

**(6) Topics**

See p29

★ **My favourite food is...** Hand out previously learnt *Big Picture Code Cards*. Have ready all the *Vocabulary Cards* that display foods (for letters you have already taught). Show one at a time and Play 'Favourite foods': My favourite food is cake. Who am I? / My favourite food is yoghurt. Who am I? / My favourite food is eggs. Who am I? etc... The child with the matching *Card* stands up and says: I'm Clever Cat. I like cake. Ask each child: **What is your favourite food?** (They can draw it later in their *Workbooks*.)

★ **Student Book & CD** Page 60

**(7) Review & pair work**

See p29

★ **Workbook** Pages 30 and 31. Children could attempt page 30 in pairs.

# Lucy Lamp Light & Vicky Violet

Lesson 16

## TEACHING OBJECTIVES:

✔ **Ii** and **vV** letter shapes and sounds
✔ Lucy Lamp Light's words: lamp, lighthouse, leg
✔ Vicky Violet's words: vase, vegetables, van
✔ Oral vocabulary: bedroom, sitting room, kitchen, bathroom

## YOU'LL NEED:

✔ Verb cards ⑥
✔ Also: See the checklist on page 35

## 1 Keywords: lamp, vase

See p16

★ **What's in the box?** Try to use a real **lamp** and **vase**. It's a lamp. The lamp makes light. It's a vase. I can put flowers in the vase. After saying each keyword together a few times, choose children to find a **lamp** and a **vase** filled with flowers on the Wall Frieze.

## 2 Letter sounds

See p17-1

★ **LLL & VV** Can you find a lamp on the wall frieze? No? Can you find a girl with a yellow hat (like a lamp!) on her head? Good! This is Lucy Lamp Light. (When she smiles, Lucy's face lights up like a lamp!) Can you find a vase? Good! This is Vicky Violet and her vase of flowers (called violets). How many violets can you count? (Five)

★ **Sounds** Lucy Lamp Light 'lll…'; Vicky Violet, 'vvv…'.

★ **Actions** Teach both Action Tricks (pages 82-83).

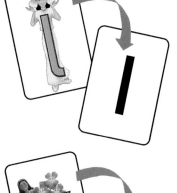

★ **Review** Do a 'Quick Dash' (page 19) through all the letter sounds and actions you have taught so far.

★ **Alphabet Songs** Sing the songs and show the Big Picture Code Cards.

★ **Picture-code** Children add picture details to plain letters.

## 3 LLL & VV's words

See p20-2

★ **Present** Use Vocabulary Cards to introduce: **lamp**, **lighthouse**, **leg**, **vase**, **vegetables** and **van**. Ask children whether each word starts with LLL's 'lll…' sound or VV's 'vvv…' sound before you put it in a sentence, e.g. Lucy Lamp Light lives in a lighthouse. Vicky Violet has a violet van. etc…

★ **Use new words** Choose an activity from the Activity Bank to give children an opportunity to use the new words. Suggestion: 'What's hiding?' (page 85).

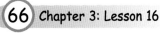

**66** Chapter 3: Lesson 16

★ **Student Book & CD** Pages 62 and 63.

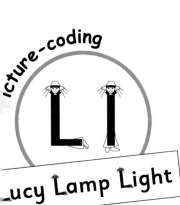

Lucy Lamp Light

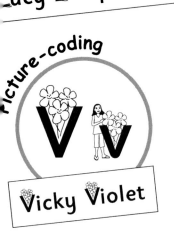

Vicky Violet

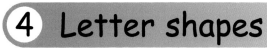

## 4 Letter shapes

See
p22-24

★ **Find the letters & form the letters** (See Lesson 13.)

★ **Capital letters** Write and picture-code lower case and capital **l** & **L** and **v** & **V** on the board. Demonstrate or translate the capital letter stories: Whenever LLL starts an important word, she takes a deep breath and gets bigger. Her legs also grow longer, so she has to kneel down with her legs on the line. Vicky Violet puts extra big vases at the start of names – like her own name - and sentences. Notice how Vicky Violet's capital letter appears TWICE in her own name. Lucy's appears THREE times!

★ **Handwriting Book** Pages 40, 41, 42 and 43

## 5 Phonemic awareness

See
p25-28

★ **Word sort & letter line** Try the cumulative role-play activity on page 25. Alternatively, choose another Revision game (pages 85-86).

★ **Workbook** Page 32 (or save it for a review activity at the end of the lesson.)

Verbs

## 6 Topics

See
p29

★ **Verbs** First revise the following verbs: **sit**, **stand**, **draw**, **paint**, **sing**, **write**, **count**, **drink**, **jump, hop** and **sleep**. Write them all on separate pieces of card in order to play 'Verb-noun mix-ups' (page 86).

★ **More verbs** Display all the *Big Picture Code Cards* you have learnt so far. Ask questions: Which Letterlander hops in the Reading Direction? (Harry Hat Man) Which Letterlander swims and dives / kicks / moves / runs / slithers in the Reading Direction?

★ **Rooms** If possible, take children on a short tour of the school in order to teach the word **sitting room**, **kitchen** and **bathroom**. Use a picture to introduce the word **bedroom**. (In preparation for *Student Book* page 64/65.)

★ **Student Book & CD** Page 64/65

## 7 Review & pair work

See
p29

★ **Workbook** Pages 32 and 33. Children could attempt both pages in pairs.

# Bouncy Ben & Jumping Jim

## Lesson 17

### TEACHING OBJECTIVES:

✔ **bB** and **jJ** letter shapes and sounds
✔ Bouncy Ben's words: ball, bed, blue
✔ Jumping Jim's words: jacket, jigsaw, juice
✔ Oral vocabulary: animals (*revision: cat, dog, horse, mouse, tiger, snake, octopus, parrot, goat, elephant, kangaroo, monkey*)
✔ Word-building: bed, red, run, fun, sun

### YOU'LL NEED:

✔ Verb cards ⑥
✔ Also: See the checklist on page 35

## ① Keywords: ball, jacket

See p16

★ **What's in the box?** Use a real **ball** and **jacket** or use the *Vocabulary Cards*. It's a ball! I can bounce the ball. Bounce, bounce, bounce. Can you bounce? Bounce like bunny rabbits together. And what's this? It's a jacket.

## ② Letter sounds

See p17-

★ **BB & JJ** Can you find a blue ball on the wall frieze? This is Bouncy Ben. He likes to bounce. Can you find a red and yellow jacket? This is Jumping Jim. Bouncy Ben and Jumping Jim are bouncing / jumping in the Reading Direction. The Reading Direction concept will help children avoid **b / d** reversals, and to curve JJ's feet behind him correctly, when forming **j** and **J**.

★ **Sounds** Use the Sounds Trick: Bouncy Ben, 'b...'; Jumping Jim, 'j...'

★ **Actions** Teach both Action Tricks (See pages 82-83).

★ **Alphabet Songs** Sing the songs and show the *Big Picture Code Cards*.

★ **Picture-code** Children add picture details to plain letters.

★ **Assessment** You have now introduced the next 6 sounds. You may like to plan to assess these 6 letter sounds <u>one week from now</u>. *Say the letter sounds in response to the plain letters*: f,r,l,v,b,j. (See page 19.)

## ③ BB & JJ's words

See p20-

★ **Present** Use *Vocabulary Cards* to introduce: **jacket, jigsaw, juice, ball, bed** and **blue**. Children decide whether each word starts with BB's short quick 'b...' sound, or JJ's 'j...' sound, before you put it in a sentence, e.g. Yes! Bouncy Ben has a big blue ball. Jumping Jim has a red and yellow jacket. etc...

★ **Use new words** Choose an activity from the Activity Bank. Suggestion: 'Order Please!' (page 84)

★ **Student Book & CD** Pages 66 and 67

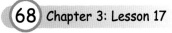

picture-coding

**B b**

Bouncy Ben

**J j**

Jumping Jim

---

**Avoid b / d reversals**
Help children to find DD &
BB in their own hands. Make
a duck head for their right
index fingers & ears and
whiskers for their left hands.
(Templates on page 107).

Animals

## ④ Letter shapes

See p22-24

★ **Find the letters & form the letters** (See Lesson 13.)

★ **Capital letters** Write and picture-code lower case and capital **b** & **B** and **j** & **J** on the board. Demonstrate or translate the capital letter stories. Whenever Bouncy Ben starts an important word, he does his 'balancing trick': he balances his blue ball between his big brown ears. When Jumping Jim starts a name or sentence, he does an extra big jump, and his head disappears in the clouds. Look! We can't see his juggling ball anymore.

★ **Handwriting Book** Pages 44, 45, 46 and 47

★ **Assessment** You have now taught the next 6 letter shapes. Plan to assess them <u>one week from now</u>. *Write letter in response to a sound*: f,r,l,v,b,j. (See page 24.)

## ⑤ Phonemic awareness & phonics

See p25-28

★ **Word sort & letter line** Try the cumulative role-play activity on page 25. Alternatively, choose another Revision game (pages 85-86).

★ **Live Spelling** Hand out *Big Picture Code Cards* **b**, **d**, **e**, **f**, **n**, **r**, **s**, and **u**. Help children to Live Spell the following words: **bed–> red–> run–> sun–> fun**. Ask the seated children to blend each resulting word.

★ **Student Book & CD** Page 69

★ **Workbook** Page 34 (or save it for a review activity at the end of the lesson.) You'll need to pre-teach the words **bicycle** and **jet** for this activity – explain that BB has a blue bicycle and JJ can jump as high as a jet!

★ **Assessment** Plan an assessment <u>one week from now</u>. Use *Activity Sheet 4: Sort words according to initial sound.* (See page 26.)

## ⑥ Topics

See p29

★ **Animals** Collect all the *Vocabulary Cards* you have taught so far. Go through them one by one asking: Is this an animal? If the answer is 'yes', ask: What is it? Put all the animal cards in a separate pile. Use them to ask questions: Which Letterlander has a horse? (Harry Hat Man) Which Letterlander is a duck? (Dippy Duck) etc... *Extension*: Put all the animal cards picture-side up on the floor. Children sit in a circle around the cards. Ask questions, such as: Which animals can fly? Which animal has eight legs? Which animal has no legs? Which animals live in the water?

★ **Student Book & CD** Page 68

## ⑦ Review & pair work

See p29

★ **Workbook** Pages 34 and 35. Children could attempt both pages in pairs.

# Walter Walrus & Fix-it Max

## TEACHING OBJECTIVES:

✔ **wW** and **xX** letter shapes and sounds
✔ Walter Walrus's words: water, window, web
✔ Fix-it Max's words: box, fox, six
✔ Oral vocabulary: trousers, dress, shirt, shoes, is wearing, Can you wash a …?
✔ Spelling pictures: wet, six

## YOU'LL NEED:

✔ Glass of water ①
✔ Also: See the checklist on page 35

## ① Keywords: water, box

See p16

★ **What's in the box?** To teach the word **water**, use a real glass of water. **It's water.** To prepare children to meet Max, say the word **box** together and emphasise the final 'k-ss' sound. Show the reverse side of the **box** *Vocabulary Card* and point to Max at the end of the word. **This is Fix-it Max!**

## ② Letter sounds

See p17-1

★ **Walter & Max** Can you find any water on the wall frieze? This is Walter Walrus and his water wells. Can you find Fix-it Max?

★ **Sounds** Use *Big Picture Code Cards* and the Sounds Trick to discover the letter sounds: Walter Walrus,'www…'. Max's sound is at the END of his name. Listen: Ma…x,  ('k-ss').

★ **Actions** Teach both Action Tricks (page 83).

★ **Alphabet Songs** Sing the ELT *Alphabet Songs*, one at a time. Show the picture-side of the *Big Picture Code Card* when you sing the character name. Show the plain letter side when you make the letter sound.

★ **Picture-code** Children add each Letterlander's picture details to plain black letters.

## ③ Walter's & Max's words

See p20-2

★ **Present** Use *Vocabulary Cards* to introduce: **water**, **window**, **web**, **box**, **fox** and **six**. Put each word into a simple sentence. Max is six years old. Max has a fox. Walter Walrus can wash windows.

★ **Use new words** Choose an activity from the Activity Bank to give children an opportunity to use the new words. Suggestion: 'What's hiding?' (page 85).

★ **Student Book & CD** Pages 70 and 71.

Picture-coding

**Walter Walrus**

**Fix-it Max**

Spelling Pictures

See p22-24

**④ Letter shapes**

★ **Find the letters & form the letters** (See previous lessons.)

★ **Capital letters** Write and picture-code lower case and capital **w** & **W** and **x** & **X** on the board. Demonstrate or translate the capital letter stories: **Whenever Walter starts a name or sentence, he takes a deep breath and gets bigger. And so does Fix-it Max, (but you'll never find his letter making his 'k-ss' sound at the beginning of words.)** Walter Walrus's capital letter appears TWICE in his own name. But Max's letter appears at the end of his name.

★ **Handwriting Book** Pages 48, 49, 50 and 51

See p25-28

**⑤ Phonemic awareness & phonics**

★ **Word sort & letter line** Try the cumulative role-play activity on page 25. Alternatively, choose another Revision game (pages 85-86).

★ **Workbook** page 36 and 37 (or save it for a review activity at the end of the lesson.)

★ **Spelling Pictures** Children picture-code each letter in the word **wet** and draw water drops all around the word. Repeat with the word **six** – children write the numeral **6** next to the word.

See p29

**⑥ Topics**

Clothes

★ **Clothes** Teach the words **trousers**, **dress**, **shirt** and **shoes** and the phrase **'is wearing'**. Review the colours **yellow**, **red**, **green**, **blue** and **orange**. Then spread FF, GG, HHM, JJ, LL, NN, TT, VV and YY *Big Picture Code Cards* on the floor and ask the following questions:

Who is wearing a yellow hat? Who is wearing a red and yellow jacket
Who is wearing a green hat? Who is wearing a green shirt?
Who is wearing yellow shoes? Who is wearing a yellow dress?
Who is wearing a violet shirt? Who is wearing orange trousers?
Who is wearing yellow trousers? Is GG wearing a green hat?
Is YYM wearing green trousers? Is HHM wearing a blue shirt? etc...

See p29

**⑦ Review & pair work**

★ **Workbook** Pages 36 and 37. Children could attempt both pages in pairs.

# Zig Zag Zebra

## Lesson 19

**TEACHING OBJECTIVES:**

✔ **z** and **Z** letter shapes and sound
✔ Zig Zag Zebra's words: zebra, zero, zoo
✔ Oral vocabulary: Review animal vocabulary
✔ Word building: Review all medial vowels: pat, pet, pit, pot; pan, pen, pin; hat, hit, hot, hut; man, men

**YOU'LL NEED:**

✔ Make a set of plain letter vowel cards ⑤

✔ Also: See the checklist on page 35

## ① Keyword: zebra

See p16

★ **What's in the box?** Use a toy zebra, zebra mask, picture or *Vocabulary Card*. It's a zebra. Look at its black and white stripes.

## ② Letter sound

See p17-1

★ **Zig Zag Zebra** Can you find a zebra on the wall frieze? Good! This is Zig Zag Zebra. Zig Zag Zebra lives in the Letterland zoo. She is very shy. (That's why she doesn't look in the Reading Direction, and why she doesn't appear in many words.)

★ **Sound** Use the *Big Picture Code Card* and the Sounds Trick to discover ZZ's letter sound: Zig Zag Zebra, 'zzz…'

★ **Action** Teach Zig Zag Zebra's Action Trick.

NB: 'zzz…' is also the sound that Sammy makes when he is sleeping in words like **is**, **his**, **boys** and **girls**.

★ **Alphabet Song** Sing Zig Zag Zebra's ELT *Alphabet Song*. Show the picture-side of her *Big Picture Code Card* when you sing her character name and the plain letter side when you make her letter sound.

★ **Picture-code** Children add Zig Zag Zebra's picture details to a plain black **z**.

★ **Assessment** You have now taught the last three **a-z** sounds. Plan to assess them <u>in the next few days</u>. *Say the letter sound in response to the plain letters*: w,x,z. (See page 19.)

Action

## ③ Zig Zag Zebra's words

See p20-2

★ **Present** Use *Vocabulary Cards* to introduce: **zebra**, **zero** and **zoo**.

★ **Use new words** Choose an activity from the Activity Bank to give children an opportunity to use the new words. Suggestion: 'All in a row' (page 84)

★ **Student Book & CD** Page 72

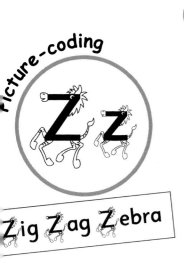

picture-coding

Zig Zag Zebra

See p22-24

## ④ Letter shapes

★ **Find the letter** Write some letters on the board, including a **z**. Can you find Zig Zag Zebra's letter?

★ **Form the letter** Write a big **z** on the board, picture-code it and air-trace it together. Start at Zig Zag Zebra's mouth. (Optional: Use her handwriting verse.)

★ **Capital letter** Write and picture-code lower case and capital **z** & **Z** on the board. Demonstrate or translate the capital letter story: **We don't see her letter very often in words, but when she does start a name or sentence Zig Zag Zebra takes a deep breath and gets bigger.** Zig Zag Zebra's capital letter appears THREE times in her name!

★ **Handwriting Book** Pages 52 and 53

★ **Assessment** You have now taught the last three **a-z** letter shapes. Plan to assess them <u>in the next few days</u>. *Write letter in response to letter sound:* w,x,z. (See page 24.)

## ⑤ Phonemic awareness & phonics

See p25-28

★ **Presenting a-z** A great way to finish off your **a-z** teaching is with a presentation of **a-z** in alphabetical order. (Alphabet Line, page 25.) Use this lesson and a few following lessons as practice sessions for a presentation, which children could share with another class or with their parents. You could even set the routine to music. To revise the **a-z** letter sounds, use the *Student Book & CD* activity on page 73.

★ **Workbook** Page 38 (or save it for a review activity at the end of the lesson).

★ **Live Reading** Review all short vowels, then play 'Vowels-go-round' (page 87) with the words **pat**, **pet**, **pit**, **pot**; **pan**, **pen**, **pin**; **hat**, **hit**, **hot**, **hut**; **man** and **men**.

Vowels-go-round

★ *Extension:* **Live Spelling** Hand out the short vowel *Cards*. Two children stand at the front of the class with enough room for a third child to stand between them. Give the end children a card each (**p_t**; **p_n**; **h_t** or **m_n**). Call out the Live Reading words (above), one at a time. The child holding the correct vowel comes up to complete the word. You could make this into a game by making a second set of plain letter vowel cards for a second team. Then, the first team to complete the word correctly scores a point.

★ **Assessment** *Activity sheet* 5 and / or *Activity Sheet* 9. (See page 29.)

## ⑥ Topics

See p29

★ **Animals** Review all the animals on the *Vocabulary Cards*. Talk about which animals might live in the Letterland zoo with Zig Zag Zebra.

## ⑦ Review & pair work

See p29

★ Workbook Page 38

# Beyond the alphabet...

The final Lesson Plans (pages 76-79) provide a brief introduction to the next level of Letterland teaching, which goes 'beyond the alphabet' and uses simple stories to explain what happens when letters change the sounds they make in words like **ship**, **fish**, **chin** and **bench**.

## Teaching digraphs & trigraphs

English has 44+ sounds (phonemes) but only 26 letters, so some of the 44+ phonemes need to be made up of two or three-letter combinations (digraphs and trigraphs). For example, in the following digraphs neither letter is making its usual sound: **sh**, **ch**, **th**, **ar**, etc.

To explain these new sounds, Letterland uses stories that build on what children already know about each letter's behaviour.

For example, one of the first things we learn about the Hat Man is that he hates noise. (That's why he doesn't wear shoes – even the sound of his own footsteps gives him a horrible headache! And it's the reason why he only whispers his usual 'hhh…' sound in most words.)

So when Sammy Snake starts hissing loudly next to the Hat Man in a word, it makes sense for the Hat Man to turn to Sammy and say, 'sh!' (the traditional English sound for hushing someone up).

Each story, like the 'sh- story', is a simple recall route to the correct sound or spelling pattern. The recall routes provided by the colourful and memorable pictograms mnemonics can be reinforced by all the senses – children act it out, they learn a song about each sound, draw it and link it to a sound and an action.

# Reviewing a-z, sh & ch

After you have completed the **sh** and **ch** Lesson Plans, you may like to use the Letterland *Activity Books* to consolidate and review all the **a-z**, **sh** and **ch** phonemes.

Use them either at the end of the Letterland ELT programme, or as a quick review of **a-z**, **sh** and **ch** at the beginning of the following year, before moving on to the next level of Letterland teaching.

## Alphabet Sounds Activity Book

Reviews **a-z** letter sounds and introduces some additional vocabulary.

## Building Words Activity Book

Children use their knowledge of **a-z**, **sh** and **ch** letter sounds to build regular words and to learn some simple new vocabulary.

## Reading Words Activity Book

Children use their knowledge of **a-z**, **sh** and **ch** to read and spell regular words. Includes high-frequency sight words ('tricky words').

Visit www.letterland.com for more information on each Activity Book.

# What can I use after Letterland ELT?

If you would like to continue teaching with Letterland stories that explain other essential phonemes (**ar**, **ow**, **er**, **igh**, etc.),use the new edition *Letterland Teacher's Guide* (ISBN 0 00 715592 1) and supporting materials.

Visit our website for more details, or email us at info@letterland.com and ask for our International catalogue.

www.letterland.com

# Sammy Snake & the Hat Man: sh...

### Lesson 20

<br />

## TEACHING OBJECTIVES:

✔ **sh** sound and shape
✔ Words: shell, ship, splash, fish
✔ Word-building: shell, ship, shop, splash, fish

## YOU'LL NEED:

✔ A shell ①
✔ A green hairy hat and a Sammy Snake headband ②
✔ **sh** Card (page 111) ②
✔ List of words ③

## ① Keywords: shell, fish

<br />

See p16

★ **What's in the box?** Use a real **shell**, or a picture. It's a shell. Say it: shell, sh...shell. You could also show the **fish** *Vocabulary* Card (or use a real fish in a bowl!), and bring attention to the 'sh...' sound at the *end* of the word. Say it: fish, fi...sh, fish.

Write up the words **fish** and **shell**. Is Sammy Snake saying 'sss...' in this word? No! Is Harry Hat Man saying his 'hhh...' sound? No! Why not?

## ② sh-story, sound & action

<br />

See p17-1

*Live Spelling*

*Action*

★ **Role play** Choose two children to come to the front. Put the Hat Man's hairy green hat on one child, and a Sammy Snake headband on the other. Take the SS child off to the side a few paces (to the seated children's left). Then ask him or her to go up to the Hat Man hissing loudly: '**sss...**'. Oh no! The Hat Man hates noise! (Ask the Hat Man child to cover his ears. What will he do? (Indicate that the Hat Man should turn to Sammy and say 'sh...!')

Now give the pair the **sh** Card and say the sound together as a class, as you all make the 'sh...' action. (See page 111 for a black and white photocopiable **sh** Card.)

## (3) Phonemic awareness & phonics

See p25-28

★ **Listen & jump!** Have ready a list of words (some contain **sh**, some do not). Children stand on the edge of a rope circle or mat. Call out one word at a time. If children hear 'sh…' anywhere in the word, they jump in the circle. If the next word does not contain 'sh…' they jump back out again. (sh words: **shark**, **shoes**, **fish**, **splash**, **shop**, **ship**, **shut**, **shower**, **wash**, **wish**)

★ **Find a Hat Man** Divide the class into Harry Hat Men and Sammy Snakes. The snakes make their slithering hand movements and the Hat Men hop on one leg. Each makes their individual sound until you say: **Find a Hat Man!** Then all the Hat Men stand still. Children pair up and act out the 'sh-story', filling the room with 'sh…' sounds.

★ **Live Spelling** Help the children to Live Spell the following words:
**shop –> ship–> shin–> fish**

★ **Spelling pictures** Children picture-code and illustrate the word **fish**. Collect the pictures for their Spelling Books.

**Spelling Picture**

## (4) Review & pair work

See p29

★ **Student Book & CD** Page 74

★ **Workbook** Page 39

**Sammy Snake headband** (mount on a stiff card)

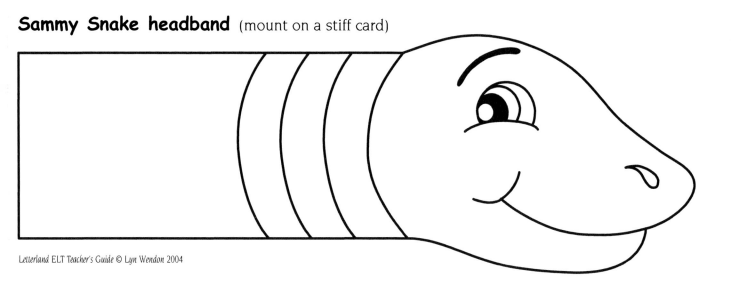

*Letterland ELT Teacher's Guide © Lyn Wendon 2004*

# Clever Cat & the Hat Man: ch...

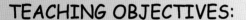

## TEACHING OBJECTIVES:

✔ **ch** sound and shape
✔ Words: chin, chick, children, bench
✔ Word-building: chin, chop, chip, chick, bench

## YOU'LL NEED:

✔ A green hairy hat and Clever Cat's ears ②
✔ **ch** Card ②
✔ List of words ③

## ① Keywords: chin, children

See p16

★ **Keywords** Write up the words **children** and **chin** and use chalk drawings to illustrate the words. **Point to your chin. Say it: chin, ch...chin. You are children. Say it: children, ch...children.** Point to the words on the board. Ask: **Is Clever Cat saying her 'c...' sound in this word? No! Is Harry Hat Man saying his 'hhh...' sound? No! Why not?**

## ② ch-story, sound & action

See p17-1

Live Spelling

★ **Role play** Choose two children to come to the front. Put the Hat Man's hairy green hat on one child, and Clever Cat's ears on the other. (They stand next to each other, as in the photo on the left). Then pretend that Harry Hat Man's very hairy hat is tickling Clever Cat's nose. **Oh no! The Hat Man's hat is tickling Clever Cat's nose! What will she do?** (Indicate that Clever Cat should politely and quietly sneeze, 'ch...!')

Now give the pair the **ch** Card and say the sound together as a class, as you all make the 'ch...' action. (See page 111 for a black and white photocopiable **ch** Card.)

Action

Live Spelling

See p25-28

## ③ Phonemic awareness & phonics

★ **Listen & jump!** Have ready a list of words (some contain **ch**, some do not). Children stand on the edge of a rope circle or mat. Call out one word at a time. If children hear 'ch…' anywhere in the word, they jump in the circle. If the next word does not contain 'ch…' they jump back out again. (ch words: **chin**, **children**, **chop**, **chin**, **cheek**, **cheese**, **chocolate**, **bench**, **bunch**)

★ **Find a Hat Man** Divide the class into Harry Hat Men and Clever Cats. The Clever Cats make her action (stroking whiskers) and the Hat Men hop on one leg. Each makes their individual sound until you say: **Find a Hat Man!** Then all the Hat Men stand still. Children pair up and act out the 'ch-story', putting their 'paws' to their noses and filling the room with polite 'ch…' sounds.

★ **Live Spelling** Help the children to Live Spell the following words: **chin–> chop–> chip–> bench**

★ **Spelling pictures** Children picture-code **ch** and illustrate the word **children**. Collect the pictures for their Spelling and Reading Books.

★ **Spelling & Reading Books** You can now compile a book for each child to take home, made up of all the 'Spelling pictures' they have made throughout the year (**cat**, **cats**, **ten**, **up**, **ducks**, **sun**, **wet**, **six**, **fish**, **children**).

You'll find a photocopiable cover for this book on page 108, and a photocopiable Reading Words List on page 109, which contains a list of all the Live Reading and Live Spelling words the children have learnt over the year. Put the cover on the front and the Reading List at the end of the booklet before you bind the pages together.

## ④ Review & pair work

See p29

★ **Student Book & CD** Page 75
★ **Workbook** Page 40

Reading Words

| | | |
|---|---|---|
| hat | nest | sun |
| hats | nut | fun |
| cat | nuts | run |
| cats | up | bed |
| sad | hot | red |
| on | hat | Fred |
| in | hit | ship |
| it | hut | shell |
| sit | man | shop |
| hit | men | chin |
| ten | pin | chick |
| net | pen | children |

# ★★★ Chapter 4 ★★★

# Appendices

# ACTION TRICKS

These actions can help children develop multi-sensory memory cues for letter sounds. There are so many supportive clues built in to Letterland teaching that the actions for each letter can be considered an optional extra. Use them according to your classes' needs.

Explain to the children that each character has an 'Action Trick' to help us remember their letter sound. To begin with, encourage children to make the letter sound each time they make the action, so that the action and sound become firmly associated. Later on, you could try using the actions in various activities. For example:

★ A child makes an action and the rest of the class says the corresponding sound.

★ Some children spell a word using actions only. The others convert the actions into sounds to build the words.

**a** Bite an imaginary apple.

**b** Shoot arms up for ears & wiggle them.

**c** Stroke whiskers across cheeks.

**d** Flap elbows like a waddling duck.

**e** Spread out hands behind ears & flap like elephant ears.

**f** Hold & direct an imaginary hose towards fire.

**g** Mime holding a tipped glass of grape juice in 'glug, glug' position.

**h** Breathe on to hand in front of mouth, OR: Put on imaginary hat.

**i** Touch fingers to thumb on the same hand as if sticky with ink & make an "icky" face.

**j** Juggle imaginary balls.

**k** Lift one arm & one foot in a **k**-shape. If sitting use arms only.

**l** Touch finger tips above head to suggest Lucy's lampshade hat.

*Letterland ELT Teacher's Guide © Lyn Wendon 2004*

 m Rub tummy.

 n Bang one fist on the other, as if hammering a nail.

 o Form round shapes with both mouth & hand & adopt a surprised look.

 p Stroke down long imaginary ears.

 q Point index finger up as if ordering "Quiet!", while saying 'qu...'.

 r Make a running movement with arms.

 s Make snake movements with hand & arm.

 t Lift arms horizontally at shoulder height in t-shape.

 u Hold up imaginary umbrella with one hand low and the other above the head.

 v Hold hands together in v-shape.

 w Flick both hands up & away as if splashing water, ending with arms in a w-shape.

 x Cross arms on chest in x-shape

 y Move hand up & down as if controlling a yo-yo.

 z Tilt head & rest against hands to mime falling asleep.

### Long vowel action
Each Vowel Man punches the air with his right hand as he calls out his name enthusiastically.

*Letterland ELT Teacher's Guide © Lyn Wendon 2004*

Display the actions in your classroom with the Action Tricks poster (see page 14 for details or visit the website at www.letterland.com).

# ACTIVITY BANK

## Activities for using new words

Most of these games can be played as whole-class activities (with *Vocabulary Cards*) or in pairs (using the photocopiable *Student Cards* on pages 91-95). If your aim is to consolidate the new alliterative words taught in Section 3, use the three new cards only.

### ✔ All in a row

This is a good 'first' activity for getting children to ask questions. Children sit in a curved row. Show the first child a *Vocabulary Card* and ask: **What's this?** Help the child to give the correct answer if necessary. (**This is a / an...**) Give the card to the child. The child then turns to the next person in the row and asks: **What's this?** This activity goes on until the last child has answered the question. He or she then goes to the front of the row for a new card.

### ✔ Draw and say

Start drawing an object on the board. Children must guess what it is: **It's a duck!** Let them take turns at drawing objects too.

### ✔ Flash cards

Flash a *Vocabulary Card* or number card quickly in front of the children. **Is this a (cat / dinosaur / apple)? Is this the number (ten)?** etc. Children respond 'yes' or 'no'. Start off slowly to make sure the children know the words. Make sure you also include questions where the answer is 'no!'

### ✔ Guess the word

Hold a *Vocabulary Card* behind your back and ask: **What is it?** Children guess the word: **It's a dinosaur!** Alternatively, divide the class into two teams, and give each child a chance to guess. Keep score of correct guesses on the board. You can also use this activity to practise numbers and colours.

### ✔ Listen and jump!

Have ready a list/s of words – some words contain the target sound and some do not. Children stand on the outside of a rope circle or mat. Choose a target sound and say it together. Call out one word at a time. If the word starts with the target sound, children jump into the rope circle or on the mat. If the next word you read starts with the target sound, they stay where they are. If not, they jump back out.

### ✔ Mood words

Teach a few mood words, for example: **happy**, **sad** and **angry**. Say each 'new word' (e.g. **cat**, **cake**, **car**) in either a happy, sad or angry tone. Children call out: **Happy cake!** or **Sad cake!** also with the same expressions.

### ✔ Order please!

Hand out the three new *Vocabulary Cards* to three children. Call out the three words in any order. Children with the cards line up in the same order as called. The rest of the class decide if they are in the correct order. Call out the cards in a different order, and repeat.

### ✔ Pass the cards

Play some music while children pass a few *Vocabulary Cards* around in a circle. When the music stops, the children who are holding the cards must say what they are holding. If they cannot, they may give it to someone else. You could also use real objects instead of cards.

## Roll the ball

Children sit in a circle. Ask a child to show everyone a *Vocabulary Card* and say the word. Roll a ball to another child. Ask the child to say the word. The child rolls the ball to another child who says the word. After 4 or 5 rolls introduce a new word.

## Shuffle cards

Display three *Vocabulary Cards*, picture side up. Then turn them over and shuffle them three times. Ask: **Is this the ...?** or **Where's the ...?** or **What's this?** Then let children play in pairs with *Student Cards*.

## What's hiding? / Who's hiding?

Place one *Vocabulary Card* behind another and slowly reveal the back card. Ask: **What's this? / Who's hiding...?** Do this as a class activity. If children have their own sets of *Student Cards*, let them play in pairs or groups.

## What's missing?

Display some *Vocabulary Cards*. Have children close their eyes. Then take one away and ask: **What's missing?** Do this as a class activity. If children have their own sets of *Student Cards*, let them play in pairs or groups.

# Review activities

Use these whole-class activities for reviewing a selection of character names, previously taught vocabulary, or letter sounds.

## Actions game

Hold up a *Big Picture Code Card*. Children make the letter sound and action. After you have been through all the letters you have introduced so far, try the sequence again, but more quickly. (A full list of actions is on pages 82-83.)

## Character names chant

Give each child a *Big Picture Code Card*. The child with the Clever Cat card starts. Then go around the class in order without missing a beat.

Child: **You say 'Clever'.** (points to class)
Class: **You say 'Cat'.** (points to child)
Class: **Clever**
Child: **Cat**
Class: **Clever**
Child: **Cat**

## Eight cards

Display eight *Vocabulary Cards* on the board, picture side showing. Say all the words in order. Turn over one card and say the eight words again. Continue turning over one card at a time until all the cards are turned over. The challenge is for everyone to say them all from memory.

## Fishing for cards

Make a fishing rod with a magnet, a piece of string, and a small stick. Put a large paper clip on each *Big Picture Code Card* and lay them face down on the floor. Give each child a chance to fish for a card. Ask: **Who is it?** Then ask the child to perform the gesture for that character while making its sound. Ask the child how many words they know that begin with that sound. Allow the other children to help. You can also remind them of words.

## Going shopping

Two children form an arch. Hand out *Vocabulary Cards* to half of the remaining children. The other half take turns to go through the arch, one at a time. Each child chooses three things that s/he wants to buy. If the child can name the picture, s/he can buy it (take the card).

## Guess the word

Give each child a turn to come to the front and choose a *Vocabulary Card* from a box. The child hides it while saying the first sound of the word. The class must repeat the sound and then guess what's on the card.

## Human sound machine

Choose three children to stand facing the class and give them each a small card with a different letter written on it. Don't let the rest of the class see these cards. Then give another child an object. When the child with the object taps one of the children with a card on the head, the child says his or her letter sound. The object is given to the child whose sound starts the name of the object.

## Knock, knock

A: **Knock, knock.**
B: **Who's there?**
A: **I like fishing.**
B: **You are Firefighter Fred!**

## Miming games

One child goes to the front. Show a *Vocabulary Card* to the rest of the class. The class mimes that word and the child must guess the word. Use words that you want to review and can be acted out. Alternatively, show a *Vocabulary Card* to one child and ask him or her to mime it for the class.

*Variation*: Call out the sound for each letter you have taught. The children respond with the gesture you taught to accompany that sound.

## Order please!

Give each child a *Vocabulary Card*. Call out a series of words. Children with those cards must line up in the correct order. The rest of the class decides if they are in the correct order. Repeat with a new set of words.

## Sound box

Place a *Big Picture Code Card* for each Letterland character you have taught so far in a box labelled the 'Sound Box'. Throughout the day, ask different children to take out a card and hold it up. The rest of the class should call out the sound it makes in words.

*Variation*: You could have separate boxes with *Vocabulary Cards* and written words for reviewing oral and reading vocabulary.

## Sound pops

Give each child a *Big Picture Code Card*. Call out a letter sound. The child or children holding the matching *Big Picture Code Card* pops up and says, for example: **Firefighter Fred says fff...** or **Munching Mike says mmm...**

## Verb-noun mix-ups

Have a pile of *Vocabulary Cards* (nouns) and a pile of verb cards. (You can make these by writing simple verbs on pieces of card.) Pick up one of each and ask: **Can a (noun) + (verb)?** For example: **Can a cake jump?** If the answer is 'no', ask: **Who can jump?** (Jumping Jim)

## What do you see?

Two children form an arch. Half of the children stand on one side of the arch and hold *Vocabulary Cards*. The other children go through the arch one at a time. For each one, chant: **Let's go to Letterland, 1, 2, 3. Let's go to Letterland, what do you see?** The child who went through the arch then says all the words s/he knows that are on the *Vocabulary Cards*, which the other children are holding.

## Who likes...?

Give each child a *Big Picture Code Card*. Show one *Vocabulary Card* at a time. Ask: **Who likes (cake)?** The child with the corresponding *Big Picture Code Card* must put up their hand and say, for example: **Clever Cat likes cake.**

# Word-building & reading games

Use these games to consolidate letter sounds and to develop word-building and reading skills.

### ✔ Vowels-go-round

Two children hold *Big Picture Code Card* **h** and **t** (or **p __ t; p__n; m__n; d__g** etc…). Five children line up with each of the short vowels (or as many as you have taught so far.) The vowel children take turns to appear in the middle position, e.g. **hat, hot, hit, hut.** The rest of the class blends the sounds to read the word.

### ✔ Silly questions

Give each child a **yes** and a **no** card. Set out the questions below on pieces of card, or write them on the board, one at a time. Hold up / write up a silly question. Ask the children to read the question and answer it by holding up their **yes** or **no** card. To help children read the character names, remind them of the 'Character Names Trick': each Letterlander does the trick of appearing TWICE as their capital letter in their own name.

**Is Bouncy Ben a dog?**
**Is Bouncy Ben a cat?**
**Is Bouncy Ben red?**
**Is Clever Cat a cat?**
**Is Dippy Duck a dog?**
**Is Dippy Duck a cat?**
**Is Dippy Duck a dog?**

# Recognising letters

Use these activities for letter recognition practice.

### ✔ Letter hunt

Give each child an enlarged piece of newspaper or magazine. Ask them to look for a particular letter and circle it each time they find one.

### ✔ Ring the words

Write a list of words on the board. E.g. **frog, sun, cat, flower, fish, apple, fire**. Ask a child to circle the words that start with Firefighter Fred's letter, or Sammy Snake's letter, etc.

# Additional pair work activities

Children use Student Cards to play these games in pairs. You could set up a variety of 'work stations' for the children to visit. Otherwise, children could all play these games at their desks.

### ✔ Grouping

Give children a set of cards for some or all the pictogram characters and words they have learnt so far. Ask them to group the words with the pictogram character according to initial sound.

### ✔ Matching upper & lower case letters

Give children a set of *Student Picture Code Cards* for all the pictogram characters they have learnt so far, as well as a matching set of capital letters. Ask them to match the picture-coded lower case letter to the plain uppercase letter.

## Memory game

Children play in pairs with two sets of *Student Cards*. Mix up the cards and place them picture side down on the desk or floor. Children may turn over two cards at a time. If they match, they may keep the pair. If not, the cards are turned picture side down again and they try to remember where the card is.

The child with the most pairs wins. This same game can be used to practice counting and colours. Children make their own coloured squares.

*Variation*: Use the game to practise plurals by having the children say: **Two cats, two ants...** etc, every time they discover a pair.

Alternatively, use for reading practice by making a set of cards with regularly spelled words to match a selection of the picture cards.

## Pair testing

One partner in a pair holds up a series of cards for the other to name. Ideally, a less advanced child tests his/her partner first. By the time it is his own turn, more of the words are familiar.

## Snap

Each child has their own pile of *Student Cards* for the words and character names to be reviewed. Each child takes a turn putting a card down. If two children put down matching cards, one after the other, they must call out the name of the character or word on the cards. The first to call out the word takes the whole pile of cards and the game continues. Make sure children's names are on the backs of their cards. Play in groups of four.

*Variation*: Use the game for reading practice by using one set of written words to match with one set of picture cards.

# COSTUMES & PROPS

| | |
|---|---|
| **Annie Apple** | Apple leaf hat; red t-shirt |
| **Bouncy Ben** | Big, brown ears |
| **Clever Cat** | Yellow ears |
| **Dippy Duck** | Headband with picture of Dippy Duck's head |
| **Eddy Elephant** | Elephant ears |
| **Firefighter Fred** | Firefighter helmet; hose; raincoat |
| **Golden Girl** | Long blond ponytail made of wool; green glasses |
| **Harry Hat Man** | Hairy green hat or hat picture on a headband |
| **Impy Ink** | Ink bottle on headband; Rainbow striped t-shirt |
| **Jumping Jim** | Jeans jacket or a red & yellow jacket |
| **Kicking King** | Crown and cape |
| **Lucy Lamp Light** | Lampshade hat |
| **Munching Mike** | Cardboard monster mask covered in foil, or headband |
| **Noisy Nick** | Toy hammer & tinfoil nails |
| **Oscar Orange** | Orange face on headband |
| **Peter Puppy** | Long droopy ears |
| **Quarrelsome Queen** | Crown & cape; plain 'royal' umbrella |

| | |
|---|---|
| **Red Robot** | Square, red cardboard headgear; red sack |
| **Sammy Snake** | Snake headband |
| **Talking Tess** | Headphones & phone |
| **Uppy Umbrella** | Small umbrella hat or real umbrella |
| **Vicky Violet** | Violet t-shirt; flower necklace or headband |
| **Walter Walrus** | Grey flippers |
| **Fix-it Max** | Toy tools and cap |
| **Yellow Yo-yo Man** | Yellow cap; yellow t-shirt; yellow yo-yo |
| **Zig Zag Zebra** | Ears on headband; black & white-striped clothing |

## Vowel Men

| | |
|---|---|
| **Mr A** | Red & white striped apron |
| **Mr E** | Top hat featuring the letter **e** |
| **Mr I** | Ice-cream cone made of rolled up paper |
| **Mr O** | White beard |
| **Mr U** | Official hat |

*Clever Cat's Costume Box*

Name _____

# PUPIL RECORD SHEET 1

| Early outcomes | a | b | c | d | e | f | g | h | i | j | k | l | m | n | o | p | q | r | s | t | u | v | w | x | y | z |
|---|---|---|---|---|---|---|---|---|---|---|---|---|---|---|---|---|---|---|---|---|---|---|---|---|---|---|
| Say the letter sound in response to plain letter | | | | | | | | | | | | | | | | | | | | | | | | | | |
| Sort words according to initial sound | | | | | | | | | | | | | | | | | | | | | | | | | | |
| Match uppercase and lower case letters* | | | | | | | | | | | | | | | | | | | | | | | | | | |
| Extension outcomes | a | b | c | d | e | f | g | h | i | j | k | l | m | n | o | p | q | r | s | t | u | v | w | x | y | z |
| Write letter in response to picture | | | | | | | | | | | | | | | | | | | | | | | | | | |
| Write letter in response to sound | | | | | | | | | | | | | | | | | | | | | | | | | | |

*See page 87

Letterland ELT Teacher's Guide © Lyn Wendon 2004

Name _____

| Assessment outcomes | Read and spell a selection of regular words | |
|---|---|---|
| hat | nest | sun |
| hats | nut | fun |
| cat | nuts | run |
| cats | up | bed |
| sad | hot | red |
| on | hat | Fred |
| in | hit | ship |
| it | hut | shell |
| sit | man | shop |
| hit | men | chin |
| ten | pin | chick |
| net | pen | children |

Letterland ELT Teacher's Guide © Lyn Wendon 2004

## Student Cards &
## Cut-outs for Activity Sheet 1

## Additional Student Cards:

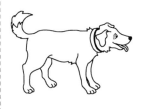   

STUDENT CARDS & CUT-OUTS

Student Cards &
Cut-outs for Activity Sheet 2

Additional Student Cards

*Letterland ELT Teacher's Guide © Lyn Wendon 2004*

*Letterland ELT Teacher's Guide © Lyn Wendon 2004*

# y,g,e,u,k,q

## STUDENT CARDS & CUT-OUTS

Student Cards &
Cut-outs for Activity Sheet 3

Additional Student Cards

# f,r,l,v,b,j

STUDENT CARDS & CUT-OUTS

### Student Cards &
### Cut-outs for Activity Sheet 4

### Additional Student Cards

*Letterland ELT Teacher's Guide © Lyn Wendon 2004*
*Letterland ELT Teacher's Guide © Lyn Wendon 2004*

Student Cards

Name _____

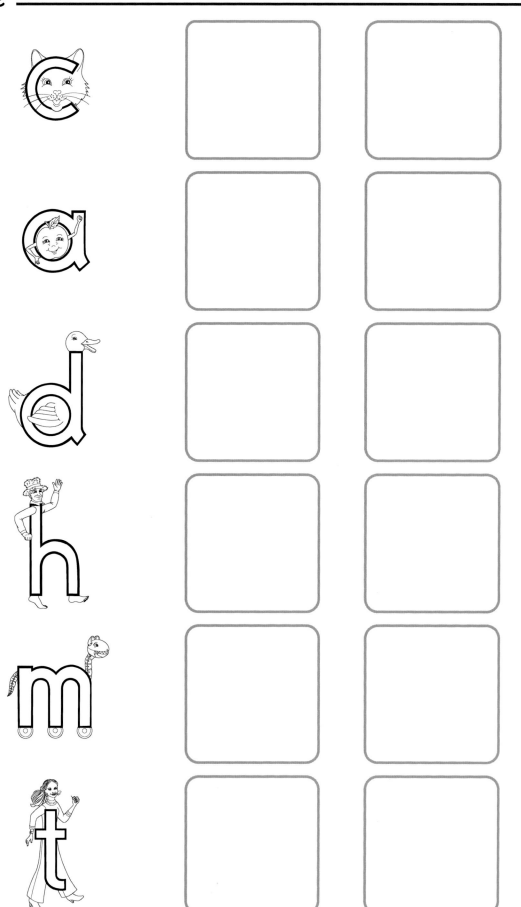

Assessment outcome: Sort words according to initial sound: c,a,d,h,m,t

Letterland ELT Teacher's Guide © Lyn Wendon 2004

Name _____

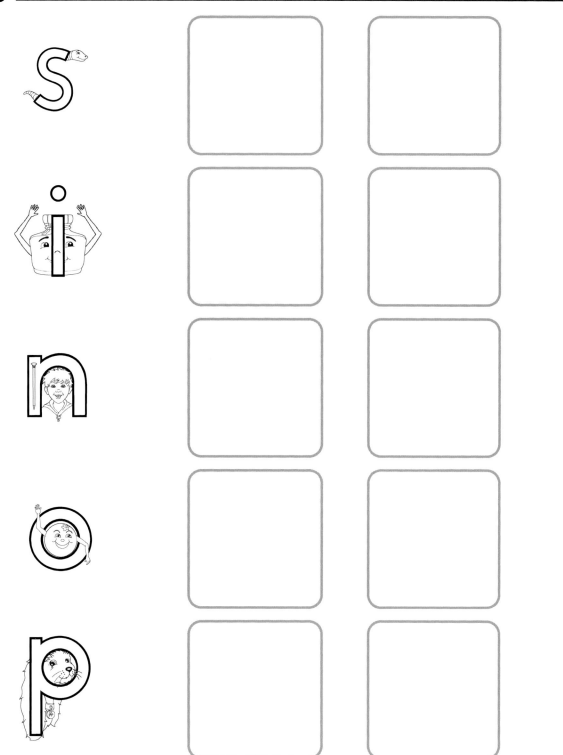

Name _____

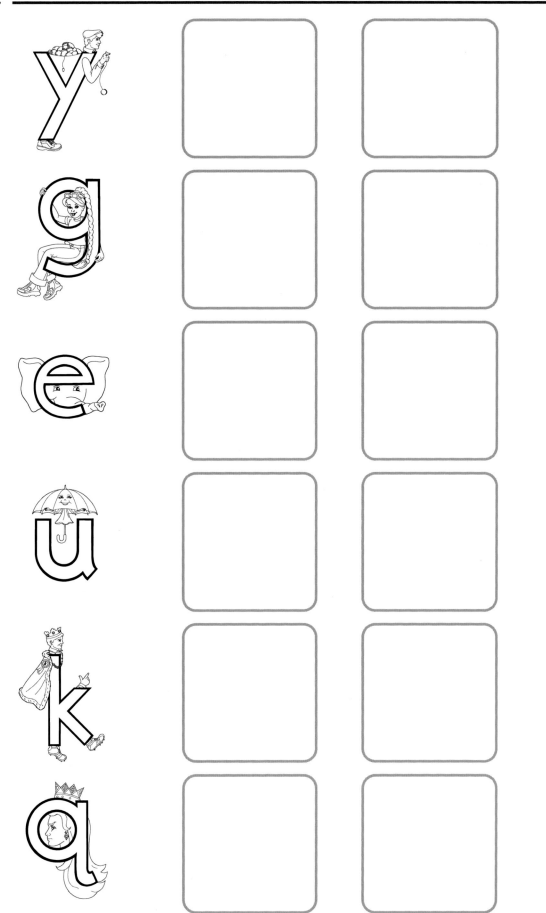

**Assessment outcome:** Sort words according to initial sound: **y,g,e,u,k,q**

Name _____

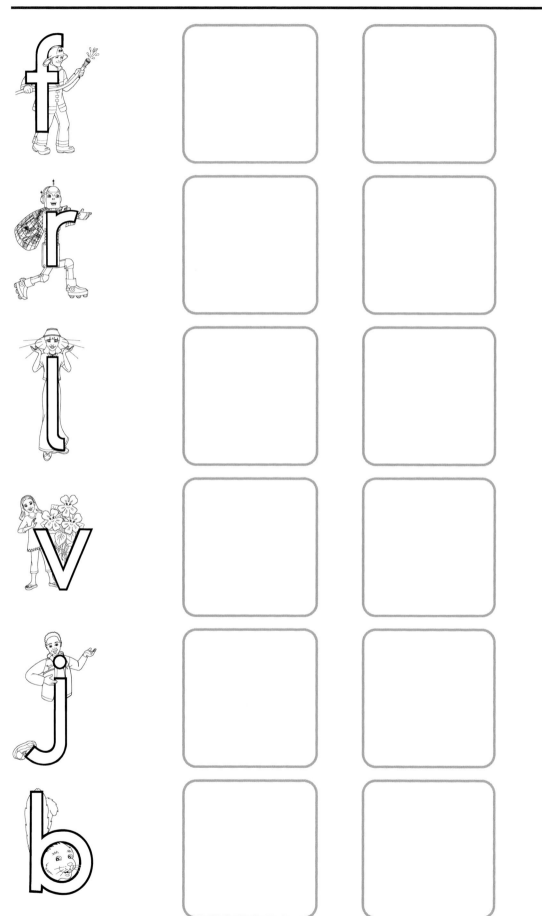

Assessment outcome: Sort words according to initial sound: **f,r,l,v,j,b**

Letterland ELT Teacher's Guide © Lyn Wendon 2004

Name _____

---

Circle the objects that END with Max's 'k-ss' sound.

---

Circle the objects that start with Walter's 'www...' sound.

  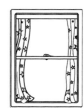

---

Circle the objects that start with Zig Zag Zebra's 'zzz...' sound.

---

**Assessment outcome: Sort words according to initial / end sound: x,w,z**

*Letterland ELT Teacher's Guide © Lyn Wendon 2004*

Name _____

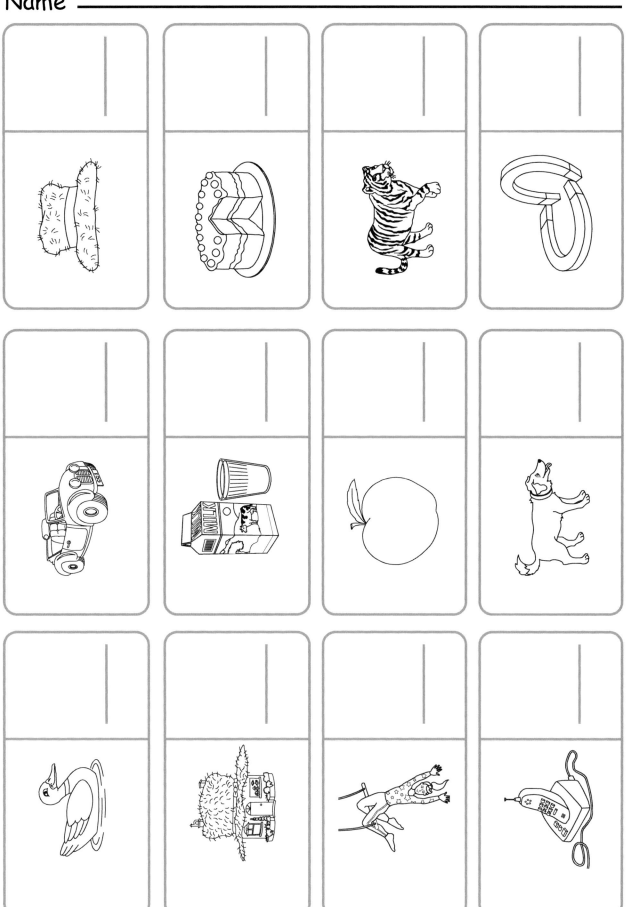

Assessment outcome: Write initial letter in response to picture: **c,a,d,h,m,t**

*Letterland ELT Teacher's Guide © Lyn Wendon 2004*

Name _____

Assessment outcome: Write initial letter in response to picture: **s,i,n,o,p**

*Letterland ELT Teacher's Guide © Lyn Wendon 2004*

Name _____

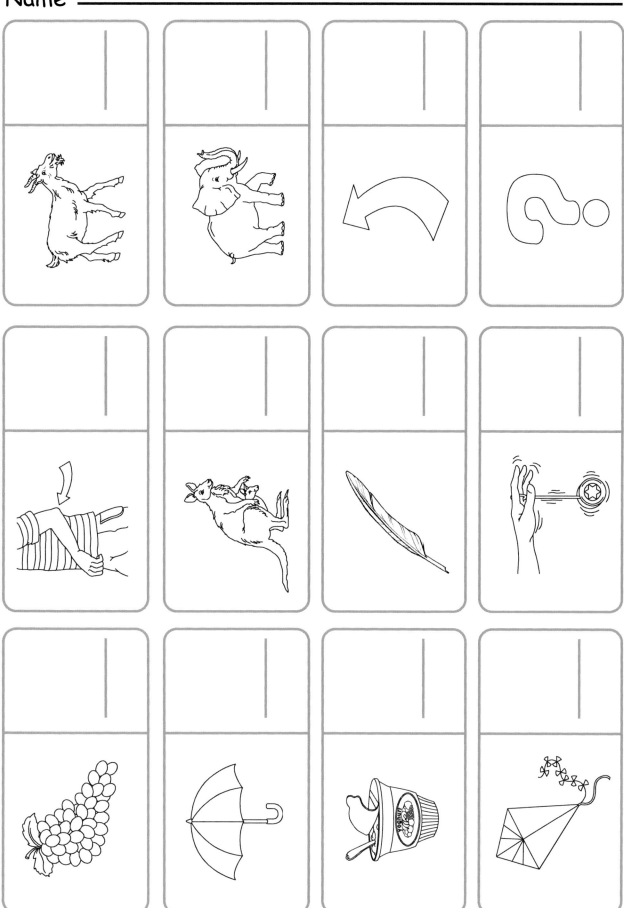

Assessment outcome: Write initial letter in response to picture: **y,g,e,u,k,q**

*Letterland ELT Teacher's Guide © Lyn Wendon 2004*

Name _____

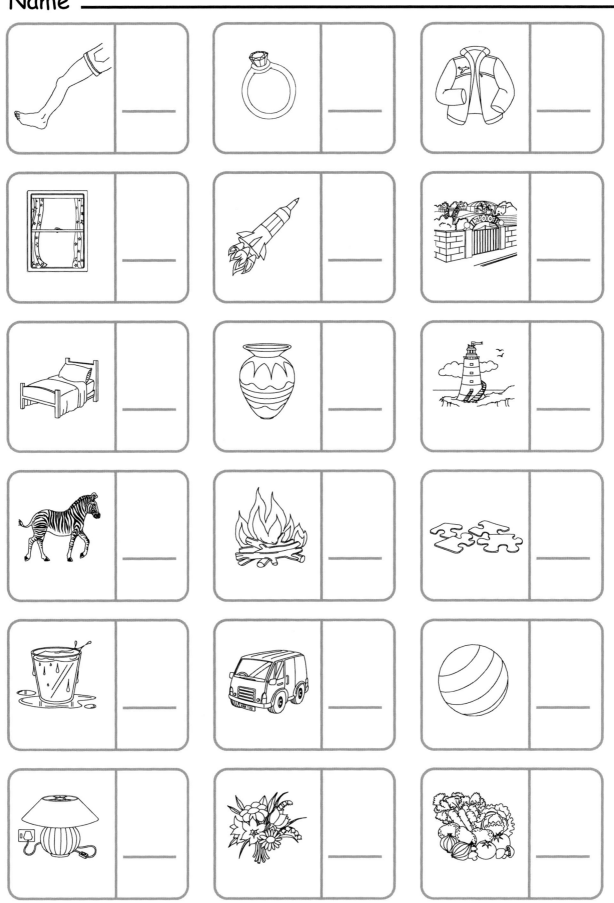

**Assessment outcome: Write initial letter in response to picture: f,r,l,v,b,j,w,z**

*Letterland ELT Teacher's Guide © Lyn Wendon 2004*

| | |
|---|---|
| Annie Apple | Noisy Nick |
| Bouncy Ben | Oscar Orange |
| Clever Cat | Peter Puppy |
| Dippy Duck | Quarrelsome Queen |
| Eddy Elephant | Red Robot |
| Firefighter Fred | Sammy Snake |
| Golden Girl | Talking Tess |
| Harry Hat Man | Uppy Umbrella |
| Impy Ink | Vicky Violet |
| Jumping Jim | Walter Walrus |
| Kicking King | Fix-it Max |
| Lucy Lamp Light | Yellow Yo-yo Man |
| Munching Mike | Zig Zag Zebra |

# The

# the

 **is**

 **in**

 **on**

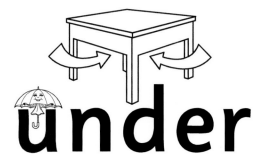 **under**

# DD & BB FINGER PUPPETS

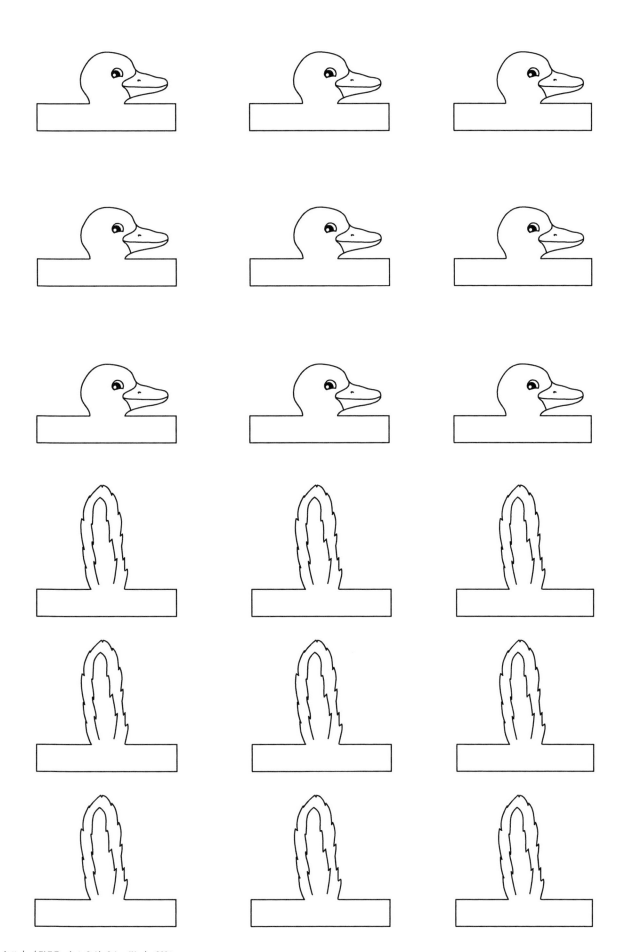

# My Spelling & Reading Book

My name is _____

# Reading Words

| | | |
|---|---|---|
| hat | nest | sun |
| hats | nut | fun |
| cat | nuts | run |
| cats | up | bed |
| sad | hot | red |
| on | hat | Fred |
| in | hit | ship |
| it | hut | shell |
| sit | man | shop |
| hit | men | chin |
| ten | pin | chick |
| net | pen | children |

# WALL MURAL TEMPLATES

## Clever Cat's picnic mural

If you'd like to display the children's first attempts at picture coding, you could stick some of their **c**-shapes on to a cat's picnic mural. The children will enjoy helping you to paint or make a country scene, showing a picnic laid out on a rug.

## Annie Apple's orchard mural

Make or paint a simple mural, showing one or more large apple trees. Leave space for Mr A to be added later. Let the children add their picture-coded **a**'s.

## Dippy Duck's duckpond mural

Prepare a mural scene of Dippy Duck's duckpond and choose some of the children to stick their picture-coded ducks in the pond. Put an arrow above the mural so that the children can see how ALL of the ducks are swimming in the Reading Direction.

Reading Direction

# GLOSSARY

**alliteration/alliterative words** A series of words with the same initial sound. E.g. Bouncy Ben's alliterative words are: **b**ed, **b**all, **b**lue

**blending** The process of combining phonemes to form a word.

**consonant** All alphabet letters except vowels **a,e,i,o,u**. The letter **y** can represent a consonant sound (**y**es) or a vowel sound (happ**y**).

**digraph** Two letters representing one phoneme: **sh**ip; c**ar**; b**oa**t; tr**ai**n

**direct teaching** Present and practise vocabulary explicitly.

**ELT** English Language Teaching: an umbrella term that incorporates ESL, EFL, EAL (S=Second, F=Foreign, A=Additional)

**high-frequency words** The most frequently occurring words in written texts, which children are usually taught to recognise on sight (e.g. a, the, this, that, he, she).

**indirect teaching** The teacher uses a controlled set of vocabulary and structures consistently throughout the lessons, in an effort to expand children's 'listening vocabulary'.

**listening vocabulary words** and sentences that children understand but which they are not expected to produce immediately.

**mnemonic** A device designed to make complex information more memorable.

**multi-sensory** A teaching approach that engages many senses as possible in an effort to address multiple intelligences; store information in the long-term memory and create multiple recall routes.

**PCC** Picture Code Card

**phonemic awareness** The ability to hear, identify and manipulate the individual sounds (phonemes) in spoken words.

**pictogram** A visual image designed to carry information. Each Letterland pictogram carries information about a letter's sound, shape, directionality and behaviour in words.

**reading/spelling by analogy** Analogy is the perception of similarity between two things; relating something known to something new. This means using known spellings to read or spell unknown words: night / right / sight-light / fright.

**regular words** Words that can be sounded out using each letter's usual sound: **cat, dog, in, on, handstand**

**segmenting** The process of breaking up a word into its individual phonemes.

**spelling pattern** The letters that represent a phoneme. Some phonemes have many different spelling patterns: d**ay**, n**a**m**e**, tr**ai**n, **eigh**t, gr**ey**, v**ei**n

**structures** Every sentence has a grammatical structure. The sentence: **Where is the cat?** has the following structure: (preposition) (verb) (article) (noun). Children can replace the noun with any other noun they know, to create many more sentences. Learning just a few grammatical structures can greatly increase children's listening and speaking vocabulary.

**trigraph** Three letters representing one phoneme: high; hear

**vowels** The five vowels, **a**, **e**, **i**, **o**, **u** can represent short or long sounds (c**ă**t, c**ā**ke). The letter **y** can also represent vowel sounds (fl**y**, ver**y**, bic**y**cle). Every syllable contains a vowel. It may be represented by one or more letters, including consonants (r**ai**n, st**ar**t, n**ow**).

**vowel men** The Letterland term for long vowels.